TRAVELS AROUND AMERICA

TRAVELS AROUND AMERICA

Harrison E. Salisbury

Walker and Company   New York

A portion of this book was first published in *Esquire* magazine.

First published in the United States of America in 1976 by the Walker Publishing Company, Inc.

Published simultaneously in Canada by Fitzhenry & Whiteside, Limited, Toronto.

Book design by Marsha Picker

ISBN: 0-8027-0549-9

Library of Congress Catalog Card Number: 76-16306

Printed in the United States of America.

10 9 8 7 6 5 4 3 2 1

To Sue and Lawrence Brooks

Acknowledgments

For their particular help in making *Travels Around America* possible, I want to express my indebtedness to the following: Melvin and Linnea Frank; Mae Rockne Cruys; Richmond and Edna Kent; Janet Salisbury; Don Erickson; Tony Salisbury; W. B. Jones; Mildred Osgood; the late Sue M. Salisbury; Mary Mebane; Werner Thiers; Cecil Roberts; Samuel Walker, my publisher; Wilson Gathings, my editor; and especially to the talented photographers Ian Patrick and Rudolph Janu.

H.E.S.

TRAVELS AROUND AMERICA

Fresh and strong the world we seize, world of labor and the
 march,
Pioneers! O pioneers!
                    —*Walt Whitman*, LEAVES OF GRASS, *1865*.

I N LATE AUTUMN New England lies naked under a steel sky,
the russet-and-gold of October stripped from granite mountains. The winds tear at the shrunken window frames of the
old red brick factories and skud leaves across the lawns of the
electronic labs on Route 128.

This is the time of year when Hiram Salisbury, yeoman of
Chepachet, Rhode Island, heaped earth around his plank-sided
house to secure it against winter winds. He had already put by
his winter's supply of potatoes, husbanded his apples for the
sauces of January and February, and begun to assemble his
stocks of men and women's shoes, cotton yardgoods and
woolens, thread and notions for a winter's trip of peddling and
carpentry, westward to Lake Erie.

No one today heaps earth mounds around the houses of
Chepachet. Nor do they put down vegetables in root cellars.
They fit their aluminum storm windows into the prefab frames
of split-levels and park the Skee-dos beside the garage prepared
for the first snowfall. There are no cutters in the broad-beamed
barns, no one remembers how to cut runners from hickory sap-
lings and armor them with steel ready to course behind sorrel
mares and dapple geldings. The sorrels and dapples are gone.

So are most of the broad-beamed barns. So are men like Hiram who would build you a sleigh for $17.69 and take your note for his pains.

On this day when the steel sky of New England is suspended over the whole country, I toss a stenographer's notebook into my briefcase, cab out to JFK, walk down the cantilever into the American 707 and transept the continent in six and a half hours. All the way to Los Angeles I fly under the metal grain of the single sky, watching from the window—New York's steel spires and glass boxes, Verrazano bridge, the soft barriers of the Appalachians moving toward me in pure morning light and then flattening, broader and broader, into that sea of land which Bryce proclaimed was meant by destiny to be the home of one people and De Tocqueville called "the most magnificent habitation ever prepared by God for man," the watershed of the Mississippi, the valleys of the Ohio and the plainslands of the Missouri, a continent in itself as surely designed for America's use as a woman's womb for the seed of humanity.

Not many of us *see* the American continent. We course it on concrete magistrals, directional lights flashing as we pull a steady 75–80 miles an hour ("Not a single stoplight all the way!") from coast to coast. We bestride it, cocooned at 37,000 feet in the soundproof asepsis of the Boeings. Casually we turn from highballs and paperbacks, stare a moment at the blur below and turn back to James Bond. We have seen nothing. We do not notice that a continent lies open there, six miles down.

Today I sit, notebook in hand, eyes to the window—aware. I am looking at *my* continent, *my* America. All year I have searched it out, traveling forgotten trails, sticking my head into nooks and crannies, old attics and new condominiums, talking to the old and the young, looking for my country, my American land, trying to find where it has been, where it has come, where it is going after two hundred years of success and sorrow, after twenty-five years of almost revolutionary struggle and turmoil. And perhaps I'm trying to find something of myself as well.

It seems to me that I have spent half my life searching out countries. I have roved the world and I have roved my own country. I have seen it from the badlands of the Dakotas (with my father), to the bayous of Louisiana (with Huey Long), from the Rangeley lakes of Maine (with my son) to the kaleidoscope of California (with Richard Milhous Nixon). I have seen all this in a lifetime of reporting but never as one America, the nation-continent of the world. I've never tried to take it all in.

Now I sit to the window and look down. We are crossing the Mississippi below Dubuque and I think of the upper river, the great bluffs, the hulking shoulders of sandstone, carved out by the heavy flow of the waters, the sparkling vastness of Lake Pepin, where I gathered mother-of-pearl as a child, the cottonwood sandbars, all that glorious river almost unknown to today's Americans, the very names a litany—Prairie du Chien, La Crosse, Winona, Wabasha, Red Wing, that watercourse which Anthony Trollope thought the finest in the world, greater than the Rhine, but a lost river to my generation of Americans locked to our freeway ribbons by steel umbilicals.

As I watch the land flow by, I wonder how I can tame the waves of impressions that flow over me. The land is so diverse. The emotions so strong. Not an easy task. "How are you going to put it all together," my poet son, Stephan, asks me. "I don't quite understand your plan."

I don't tell him that I don't quite understand either. I don't say what I really think—that America is bigger than any plan, too vast for a map. It sweeps me away like the great breakers that once turned me over and over on the sandy beach at Wainscott until I gasped for life. Old Bob La Follette, the radical from Wisconsin, was right when he said you could not make a plan to fit America. It was too big, too changing, too varied. "It just won't work," he told the schemers with their utopian schemes. How can I hope to grasp it? Whitman came closest to capturing it. Da Vinci might have done it on the wall of a limestone cave on the Missouri. I think of those who have tried— Tom Benton with his brush, Saint-Gaudens in marble, Sandburg in words, Copland in music, Frederick Jackson Turner in myth, Jefferson in a dream.

None of them caught it all, each grasped his own America. That is as much as I can do—see my America with my own eyes. Put it down in my own words. It will not be everyone's America. It cannot even be all of my own because the images twist and turn, dissolve and resolve again in changing form. There are a thousand thousand strands in the American tapestry. The warp and woof is beyond the art of a weaver like myself. Why is it so important to me to try to bring the focus of my country sharp-edged to my own eyes? Has the sun begun to set on the American dream? Is this the last chance for a retrospective portrait before we follow Victoria's empire into shadow and nostalgia?

I cannot believe it. I cannot believe we have aborted Nixon only to die of a septic cynicism. I will not join the doomsayers who fear a phalanx of missile-tipped American centurions wait in the wings to impose nuclear *diktat* upon the world. Nor those who see us feebly faltering into decadence.

That is not my America. I can feel my will wrestling against the concept. This is not what we have fought two hundred years to create. And yet where is hope? Does it exist only in some inner pocket of my mind? Can I document conviction that the dream has not died and that like a chrysalis it will give birth to a new glory?

Let me be honest. I cannot put it *all* together. I can offer only one man's search for signs. I can offer *my* America. Each man's America must be his own, for that is the essence of the American contract. Each of us is but part of the continent, part of the main. I have no blueprint, just some jottings on old envelopes, some penciled lines on highway maps of Rhode Island, New York and Wisconsin, some old letters, some new talk, fresh as paint. I have not penetrated each corner of the USA—and if I had, would I be much the wiser? I have not sampled white lightning with the good ol' boys of the Carolina hills nor swapped wives in Phoenix, Arizona. I have not lived a wet and freezing winter in an Oregon commune nor sat in a consciousness-raising session with methadone freaks. I have not tasted every strata of our 230 million lives.

We are a torrent, a turbulent torrent of humanity, as fractious as the world has seen, spinning like a whirlwind through twenty decades of existence. How can I capture it? Slowly it comes to me that, incredibly, I have shared one-third of our country's life, sixty-six years of the history of the United States has been my history as well. I was born when the pride of the Spanish war was still hot in American blood. Old Unk, my father's uncle, put on his blue serge suit and marched down Nicollet Avenue on Memorial Day as a survivor of Andersonville. In those days the Indians still stood at the horizon of my Minnesota land, and my father saw the great buffalo herds wallowing in grass, tall as a man's shoulder, the hides stacked beside Dakota stations of the Soo Line in quarter-mile cords like firewood. Half the years of our Republic I know close to firsthand—from my own life, my life as a reporter or by family conversation. Casting back—the lives of my father, his father, his grandfather and great-grandfather take the story to 1776 and before—four lives and my own span the country's history. My father's great-grandfather, John Salisbury, fought to establish the Republic. No commander he. Just a plain yeoman who served with Washington, there at the beginning, mustered into the Continental Army, fighting the British a while, laying down his musket to tend his crops in Rhode Island, then fighting again.

These four lives—and my own—encompass our history. They mark the path I have traced—a reporter's path—the lives, the towns, the people of towns, the memories, the growth, the tragedy, the conflict, the decay, the dreams, the disillusions, the aspirations, the delights. The cavalcade spans the continent as it spans the centuries. There are no powerful men in this saga, no Presidents, no Secretaries of State, Ambassadors to the Court of St. James's, no millionaires, no Justices of the Supreme Court, no horse thieves, no hangmen, no Princes of the cloth nor sages of learning.

This is a plain tale of plain Americans, living their lives, building their villages, raising their families, tilling the land, moving westward with restless feet, those restless feet which the novelist John P. Kennedy thought the most American of our characteristics. The American, he said, "is a migratious one. He has no root in the soil. He is devoured with a passion for locomotion. He must come and go."

So, I thought, we have come and gone, back and forth across the continent, the four generations before me. And then myself in my one-third of America's lifetime have traveled more than all the rest multiplied ten times, transitting the continent so often I cannot number the times but seldom *seeing* the continent as I see it today.

When was the first time? When I flew home from the war, flying in from the Pacific, completing my first span of the globe, flying into San Francisco from Honolulu in the sparkling dawn, the white city climbing up the banks of Telegraph Hill, Nob Hill, Russian Hill, the bridges like a queen's diamonds, and then across the country and into New York at dusk, the lights burning with a golden glow.

I better recall the trip west with Nikita Khrushchev, looking down from the plane as I do today. I rode much of the time in the cockpit with the pilot, staring out, trying to see America as it spread before the small, darting eyes of Russia's most volatile politician. I knew he didn't miss much. I knew he understood the meaning of those hours of flight across the black earth of Ohio, Indiana, Illinois, Iowa, Kansas, the Southwest. I could understand what Khrushchev saw and what he felt as America raced beneath him. It was all *chernozem*, all rich black soil like the richest of the Ukraine and all south of the latitude of the Ukraine, thousands of miles of black soil. It had sunshine and rainfall and a long growing season.

The land flowed on and on as I stared down. Now it was quarter sections of Iowa land, sixty acres on one side, three hundred sixty acres, the landscape and economy of our richest farm state. I have seen Iowa, too, with Russian eyes, first Matskevich and the Russian agricultural delegation of 1955, which clambered over the tractors, the harvesters, the great farm machinery and said in wonder at the labor-saving: "By you one man. By us one hundred!" I had been with Khrushchev on Roswell Garst's miracle farm at Coon Rapids and had watched the sparkle in Khrushchev's eyes as he saw the machines chop and hoist the mountains of corn into fodder.

What would he have given to annex Iowa to the Soviet Union, lock, stock and barrel, Garst and his farm included! Really, I wondered, was there anything grander in America than Iowa and its corn and hogs? Was there anything in electronics to beat it? Didn't it lick the Agribusiness of the Imperial Valley? Didn't it top Detroit and its production lines? Wasn't it greater than Harvard and Cal Tech? Could Emerson's genius, Lincoln Center or the Golden Gate Bridge be rated higher? Never! Iowa possessed the finest agricultural economy in the world—a match of Yankee ingenuity, field practise, hard work, advanced technology, education, capital-intensive cultivation, scientific genetics—every resource of our late twentieth-century society. The Russians had gotten first to outer space; but we were so far ahead on Buckminster Fuller's planet earth no one would ever catch up. I could not think of Iowa without confidence. Washington might wallow in crookedness and stupidity, Wall Street might go to the dogs, California to the cranks. But Iowa—I would match it against the world.

I could not help my rise of pride. The midwest was where I was born. The midwest was still where it was at. So I thought.

Kansas was coming up, no checkerboard, the wheatfields spread too widely. Ahead was Colorado. States flew past like water towers on the old Great Northern. We were entering that vast region that—not in my school geography but my father's— had been outlined vague and empty, the great American desert. Nothing there. But that was nonsense. As Josiah Strong had said the "great American desert" was "nomadic and elusive," it ever receded before advancing civilization.

Here I see the Colorado River, ballooning like an inflated condom. Monument Valley cuts through the red loess like butter and I start in recognition. I am seeing something I have seen before but not on the American continent. The red loess, I realize, is like that I saw in the mountains north of Sian, the rugged ranges which led Mao Tse-tung on the long march into his fastness at Yenan. Here below me the angles are softer, the esplanades at 22,000 feet more broad (but we flew far lower going into Yenan) and Arizona looks like a battlefield in Mars, pocked with craters.

I laugh to myself. I am remembering Leonid Brezhnev when he flew over Grand Canyon. To him it was not a geological fantasy. His comment: "My regrets. We all have these problems." He was telling us how he sympathized that we could not put the canyon to the plow. Khrushchev had been excited as a child at the Canyon. He knew the difference between agriculture and scenery.

The wind fuzzes the desert surface. Off to the right Las Vegas sprouts its pornographic morels and rectangles of agribusiness stretch brown and sullen on the Mojave. There is Lake Arrowhead, there Big Bear Lake, still in the mountain country, the lakes turquoise in the upthrust basalt, a four-lane cutting the mountain walls and carrying through the valley, where I see smoke rising on the ridges. But it is smog not smoke. I think of the proud boast of my Moscow friends: "We, too, now have smog!" A symbol of late twentieth-century progress, they, too, coming nearer the brink of eternity. The smog rides up the mountains, only the peaks are visible, black and brown, sinister mountains, dead mountains.

San Bernardino lies asphyxiating under a gray bed of smog. Everyone in Los Angeles complains the antismog devices are no good, they cost money, boost gas consumption, cut power ratios, poison the air with new chemicals, increase the smog. But everyone in the Valley says: "Thank God, we live in the Valley. No smog there." I cannot see the Valley for the smog, but now we are low enough to expose Los Angeles lifeless, or so it seems, under a thin dusting of face powder. The haze furs the city until it loses its boundaries and extrudes into vacant space, more monotone than the desert—no greens, no reds, no purples, no yellows, no primary colors.

For fifteen minutes we circle, the passengers still wired to their headsets, dozing and nodding. The city seems dead as a putrifying squid with varicose veins stapled to a plastic belly. We drop a bit and I see that the veins are freeways carved into

Los Angeles like the scars of Andy Warhol's abdomen. A child looking out the plane window screams. "It's nothing," the mother says. "We're just coming into Los Angeles."

The plane jolts to the ground and I am surprised to find the sun shining thinly, the air warm and soft. The pungent smell of eucalyptus fills my nostrils. I remember other landings in Los Angeles, the one with Khrushchev in the remote corner of the airfield where Mayor Paulson proclaimed: "Los Angeles is the City of the Impossible—where the unexpected always happens." How right he was!

I head for the Beverly Hilton. On the freeway each person is enclosed in his metallic mobile womb, ears glued to the traffic broadcasts. The Toyotas, the Datsuns, the Subarus, the Hondas, the old U.S. iron whisper past. We hit Century Boulevard and gradually drop to street level, my eyes glued to the window watching the signs: Sexual Catharsis, Sexual Relief and a plain pink stucco building with a plain pink sign: Girls. Here is an Adult Motel (porno movies on closed-circuit TV but bring your own girl) and the Institute of World Love—massive red lips in neon lights. The driver brags that Los Angeles has more special sexual attractions than any other city—places with female dwarfs, with wrestling girls, amputees, boys, even children if that's your taste. An underground porn film is making the rounds of the Bel-Air homes and the Beverly Hills viewing rooms. Very special. Made, they say, in the Argentine. It has everything, every sexual variation, human and animal and human-animal. The climax—a girl is raped, killed and butchered before the viewer's eyes. Who knows whether it is real or fake. Making a mint out here. Everyone is crazy to see it. I remember when poor Khrushchev stalked out of the 20th Century lot because he thought he was being exposed to pornography— the lovely can-can dancers with their cascades of petticoats.

The taxi pulls up to the hotel and I get out. The first time I reported on Los Angeles two agronomists took me on a long drive to Riverside to show me the danger line where orange trees would no longer grow because of smog and the line closer to the city where spinach, more sensitive than man, blackened and withered in the atmosphere Los Angeles breathed. Now Los Angeles has three classes of alerts for its schools: No. 1, No gym. No. 2, All activity restricted, children stay within. No. 3, Don't move.

Sixteen years ago I wrote as the lead of my Los Angeles

story: "I have seen the Future—and it doesn't work." Is this what 200 years of struggle and strife, courage and sacrifice, have brought us—a Pacific construct of emulsified nihilism? That I do not believe. But what *was* the path we followed, how have we gotten from there to here? Where is the real America?

I must go back to beginnings, to where America was born, to the Hirams and the Chepachets of our land.

2

The talent of a New Englander is universal. He is a good farmer, an excellent school teacher, a very respectable preacher, a capital lawyer, a sagacious physician, an able editor, a thriving merchant, a shrewd pedlar and a most industrious tradesman.
—*Francis J. Grund, 1837.*

I DON'T KNOW WHAT I expected to find at Chepachet, the place that was the beginning. In fact, when I started out I was not certain that Chepachet *was* the beginning. Town lines change, names are discarded, villages vanish. When 150 years have passed, or 175, you do not drop down on a village street and find neighbors who remember.

No one, I knew, in our times could recall Hiram Salisbury, born in 1779, three years into the Revolution, first child of John, veteran of the Battle of White Plains, still serving month on, month off, in Washington's Army. When I decided to hunt out Hiram, I was looking for an obscure, unmarried yeoman, living in Glocester, a rambling Rhode Island township jammed into the Connecticut–Rhode Island–Massachusetts triangle, where in the 1800s was located Chepachet, a lively village, the village where Hiram traded and voted and bought his nails and sugar and, sometimes, his rum.

I did not go empty-handed on my search for the beginning. On October 6, 1815, Hiram, thirty-six years old, rode his wagon

Burrillville May 8 AD 1836

Dear Father

I embrace the present opportunity to write a letter to you to inform you that I am in usual health I still reside on a part of the Old Enoch Whipple farm I keep house and my son Chauncey and my little boy Smith live with me and my little girl lives with Brother John. I find some difficulty in hiring womens help almost all our women and girls go to work in the Cotton and woolen Factories and make ~~make~~ from 2 to 3 Dollars per week besides paying their board and common farmers cant afford to pay such a price for work and get along they had better sell out and move. Uncle Heber lives with me yet he is so lame with gout and reumatism as to be hardly able to walk across the house with 2 staves. aunt Mary Butts was down here last fall from Stafford Connecticut she lives with Amasa Sweet her son in law old uncle Stephen Blackmarr I believe is yet living in Hebron in Connecticut. Brother John and wife are well they have a little Daughter 2 years old they live with father

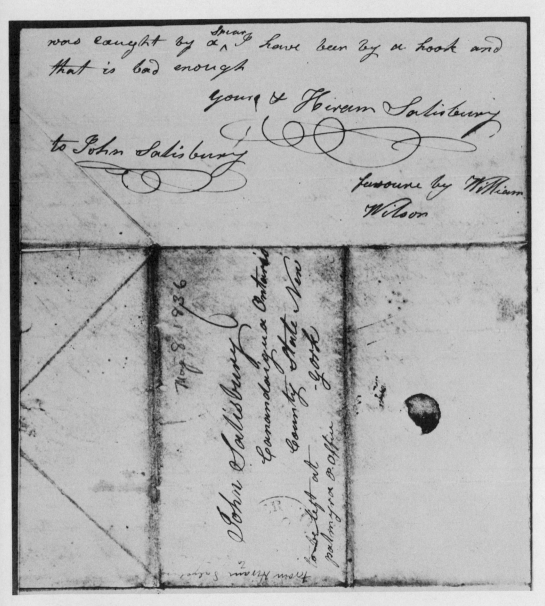

Hiram Salisbury's letter: "I do not know but I shall have to break up keeping house. All the women worth anything go to the factories and make $2 and $3 per week."

into Providence, a day's drive, and on that trip, fifteen days after the tornado of September 23, 1815, as he meticulously noted, bought a ledger of good rag paper in which to keep his day journal, his accounts, moneys spent, moneys owed, work done, travel accomplished and occasionally, very occasionally, thoughts worth preserving, observations on his own state or the state of the Union. I had that journal.

I knew that almost every year in late autumn, when the ground froze and the autumn chores were done, Hiram loaded his wagon and set off westward to Canandaigua, New York, where his father had moved in 1802 and where his brother, Amasa, my great-grandfather, now lived. Then on to Buffalo, where two other brothers, Smith Hamilton and Hezekiah Alexander, ran a bookstore and, precariously, the first newspaper to be started in that town.

It was no idyllic world in which Hiram lived. He lived in a real world of cold, mud and sweat. He did not plan his long winter odyssey to while away idle days when the earth lay fallow. It was business, pure and simple, a commercial venture, a peddling trip. Hiram loaded his wagon (I know what he loaded because he was careful to jot it all down) with cotton shirtings at five cents a yard, bed ticking, satinet yard goods (he bought at $1.20 a yard and sold for $2.00), hundreds of pounds of cotton yarn, fine shoes for men ($2.50 a pair), fine shoes for women ($1.25 a pair), slippers, overshoes, boots, candles, silk thread and notions of many kinds.

All winter Hiram carried on his peddler's trade and worked as a carpenter and cabinetmaker until spring brought him back to Rhode Island for planting and the new crop year. He was what Daniel Boorstin might have called an "upstart man," a man on the move, a man whose skills seemed to have no limit. He lived in a day when the Revolution was common experience. Half the men he dealt with had fought in it. He was a man of his time but what kind of a man was that, the first generation after Independence had been won?

I scan the journal for clues and reconstruct the post-Revolutionary American. I list his skills, one sheet of scratch paper after another. He knew every farm chore. He milked the cows and tended the calves in birth. He physicked his horse. He plowed, he planted, he cultivated, hayed, picked apples, grafted fruit trees, cut wheat with a scythe, cradled oats, threshed grain with a flail on a clay floor. He chopped the corn and put down his vegetables for winter. He made cider and built cider mills. He made cheese and fashioned cheese tongs.

He butchered the hogs and sheered the sheep. He churned butter and salted it. He made soap and candles, thatched barns and built smokehouses. He butchered oxen and constructed ox sledges. He fought forest fires and marked out the land. He repaired the crane at Smith's mill and forged a crane for his own fireplace to hang the kettle on. He collected iron in the countryside and smelted it. He tapped (mended) his children's shoes and his own. He built trundle beds, ox carts, sleighs, wagons, wagon wheels and wheel spokes. He turned logs into boards and cut locust wood picket fences. He made houseframes—beams, mortised and pegged. With six men's help he raised the frames and built the houses. He made a neat cherry stand with a drawer for a cousin, fixed clocks and went fishing. He carved his own board measures (yardsticks) and sold them for a dollar apiece. He fitted window cases, mended locks and fixed compasses. He hewed timber, surveyed the forest, wrote deeds and shaved shingles. He inspected the town records and audited the books of the Friendship Lodge, the oldest freshwater Masonic lodge in the country (still running). He chipped plows, constructed carding machines, carved gunstocks and built looms. He set gravestones and fashioned wagon hubs. He ran a bookstore and could make a fine coffin in half a day. He was a member of the State Assembly, overseer of the poor, appraiser of property and fellow of the town council. He made hoops by the thousand and also pewter faucets. For many years he collected the town taxes, bidding for the job every year and winning it until the day came when laconically he noted on June 6, 1842: "I go to Town meeting—I lost all my offices." Possibly it was because he had been spending so much time at Mistress Betsey Burlingame's, often, as he wrote, "staying the night."

I have not listed all of Hiram's skills but enough. I do not think he was an unusual man. Compare our times—match his skills against mine. I am a city man. I can run a typewriter and drive a car. With difficulty I can change a tire. I can drive a nail but not well; chop wood but not well; run a power saw but not well; fix an electric switch but not very certainly. Put me in Hiram's world and I would not last long. Put any of us down in Chepachet in the early 1800s—we might survive but it would be on the charity of our neighbors. Put Hiram down in our world. He might have a little trouble with a computer but he'd get the hang of it faster than I could cradle a bushel of oats.

Hiram got paid for every one of the skills I have listed. But seldom in money. Money was the scarcest thing. When he got a piece of currency in his hands he listed it ("three $5 bills, 1st

Bank, Buffalo, Nos 1169, 1170, 1171"). When he paid in silver he often got a premium. But Hiram lived on paper. He would give a note of $36 to the Masonic Lodge and take one from Mr. Winsor for $62.86 for doing some carpentry.

Hiram seldom was sick and when he was it was usually a chill, a fever, a flux or, later in life, a lame leg. He never saw a doctor. There is a rare record of a doctor's visit when his wife was taken sick June 20, 1832, and died within the fortnight "of mental derangement." (She prayed night after night, all night, making everyone pray with her.) Doctor Eddy came the day she fell ill and Doctor David Smith the day she died. Hiram did not report what the doctor charged but later that summer he made a cider mill for Doctor Eddy. Perhaps that was Eddy's pay. The coffin cost $5.50. Hiram did not make it.

Doctors hardly touched Hiram's life—but the deaths! Page after page of deaths. Letter after letter recording them line by line. The gravestones of wives and infant children haunt the cemeteries. Hiram was the first son of his father John's first marriage; my great-grandfather, Amasa was the second son of John's second marriage; seven children by the first wife, eleven by the second; fourteen surviving to adulthood. There are 105 graveyards in Glocester and 135 next door in Burrillville, monuments to childbed fever, consumption, pneumonia, the epidemic diseases that raged the land, typhoid, smallpox, measles. For each husband a tatter of wives—dead at twenty-three, at twenty-eight, at twenty-seven. To be a woman was an almost fatal early disease.

I check out of Howard Johnson's orange-green-white palazzo on I-95 south of Providence on a hot smoggy morning. It is eighteen miles to Chepachet, too far for Hiram to make it to Providence and back in one day. Sometimes he stopped overnight at Daniel Angell's inn, where it cost him fifty-five cents for supper, lodging and the keeping of his horse. He paid three cents in tolls. I paid no tolls but the Howard Johnson bill was $26.75 with dinner and a few phone calls.

I don't know Hiram's route but mine leads through a devastated area around the State House, across state parking fields, then by rough granite streets, past nineteenth-century mills to Route 44 and the urban fringe through Smithfield. No farms. No cattle. The country urbanized. Here and there a classic low Rhode Island house survives with framed doors and a barn on old stone foundations. The names are Italian and French-Canadian.

Slowly I drive into Chepachet. I recognized no trace of Hiram's day. He had bought nails from Sam Ross, tools and iron from E. Brown, dress goods from Burt Aldrich. He had dealings with Elisa Brown, D. Sayles, Amasa and Smith Brown and P. Walker, Sr., who ran the sawmill. His countryside was dotted with factories—the Blackstone Cotton Manufactury, A. P. Slater's mill, Quoddick factory, the Branch factory. He sometimes went to the A. Evans hotel and the iron furnace. He attended Universalist and Baptist meetings and changed money at the bank in Smithfield. He was treasurer of Friendship Lodge No. 7 of the Masons, established May 5, 1800, at Chepachet.

Of all this no trace but my heart leaps. I see a wooden store with an antique sign: Brown and Hopkins, founded 1809. Hopkins I do not know. Brown is a man Hiram did business with. But the lady who runs Brown and Hopkins is no help. She leases the store, a "genuine old-fashioned New England country store." She knows nothing about the Browns, nothing about Hiram or any other Salisbury (I found ninety-eight listed in the Greater Providence telephone book), nothing about Chepachet. But there is a lady, she says, who knows something about the town—Edna Kent. She lives just down the street on Dorr Drive. Her hobby is Chepachet and its history.

The tapes . . . Richmond Kent, Edna's husband, has more than one hundred hours of tapes . . . Silas Spink and Old Sheldon of the Mullins Mill, Elias Peckham and Leonard Sayles, Elmer Keach and Mrs. Mitchell of Iron Stone Road, Cora Kent, James Steere and John Lester Brown . . . The old names, the old memories, the old men and women of the village, recorded in their eighties or nineties. The names reach back to Hiram's journals, some of the memories are handed down from his times.

Cora Kent is speaking. She is eighty-four:
"Chepachet village was a beautiful place. The trees were maple and elm and they formed an arch over the streets at the top where they came together. It was a beautiful spot. It was such a pleasure to live here where everybody knew everybody you met on the street. Oh, it was such a pleasure. . ."
Mrs. Clifford Brown speaks. She is in her seventies. Her

father set up a power generator on his farm and provided electricity for Chepachet until Narragansett Electric bought him out in 1931:

"I remember that first night the light went on. People drove in with their horse and wagons. They stood there at Brown & Hopkins with their mouths open, just looking at that light like it was one of the seven wonders of the world.

"Chepachet village was a beautiful place. The trees were maple and elm and they formed an arch over the streets at the top. . . ."
(*Courtesy,* GLOCESTER HERITAGE SOCIETY)

"Father came home with tears in his eyes the day they tore down the old hotel that used to be the stagecoach inn. That was at the corner where the Texaco place is, right on the corner, small and built of clapboards. In those days we were one big family—the whole town."

James Steere speaks. He is eighty-eight and will not live out another winter:

"There was an awful crowd here that day—Trolley Day. It was in 1914 about the Fourth of July. Guess the biggest crowd we ever had. There was a clambake in the churchyard and a parade. A man walked ahead with a big staff, then the oxen, the teams of oxen, and people on those old-fashioned bicycles with the great big wheels in front and the little wheels in back."

Trolley Day. To celebrate the street railway which had finally reached Chepachet from Providence. The biggest day Chepachet ever had. Nothing came swiftly to Chepachet. It was a conservative community. It still is. Chepachet never let the railroad in—afraid sparks from the locomotives would set fire to the hayfields. Hay was important and this was the kind of objection Hiram would have understood. In fact, he may have joined in it. The railroad came to Providence in the 1830s and he took it for the first time in May 18, 1839 ("I take the cars and go to Boston $15.00"). But not in his lifetime nor any time after did it come much closer to Chepachet.

Hiram died in 1850. He would not have believed that Chepachet had passed its peak by his last years, although he knew that times were changing fast. Fifteen years before he had written his father in Canandaigua: "I have been very much put to it for women's help since I lost my wife. I have not had any women's help since New Years. I do not know but I shall have to break up keeping house. All the women worth anything go to the cotton and woolen factorys and make $2 and $3 per week exclusive of paying their board."

No one remembers now whether the early Chepachet mills ran on the Lowell system, a plan which provided light and airy boarding houses for the young girls and women, reading rooms and libraries, guards to protect them from the rude vulgarities of men, lectures and sermons to improve their minds. James Steere's memory went deep into the nineteenth century, but all he could recall was being told by his mother that the hours of labor in the mills were six to six and the pay ten cents an hour.

It was the mills which made Chepachet and the mills which broke it. Today in Chepachet no mill turns its wheels. A mattress factory which employed twelve persons is closed. A family furniture factory carries on in West Glocester. It has been generations since farming was really important. Three dairy farms still survive.

In Hiram's day Chepachet was a Jacksonian stronghold.

("Eaton and Walling team got beat 36 majority. Huzza for Jackson!!!!") But as far back as those alive can remember, Chepachet has been Republican. It broke the pattern in 1932 and went for FDR, but in two years slipped back to the Republicans. Now there is uneasiness. The war and Watergate have left scars. Political moorings have been loosened as the "Elephant bridge incident" shows. Its beginnings go back to Hiram's time, 1822. Somehow he failed to record it in his journal although that year he did note "a case in Bastardy, Sarah Salisbury vs Israel Wakefield," a four-day fire in the woods, the suicide of John Hanks in a small brook near Herring Pond and "a great Fight between Bull Barns and O-Tis-Hop-kins."

The elephant was named Big Bess. It belonged to one of the circuses which made a habit of halting at the Chepachet Inn. Six young men shot the elephant as it walked across the bridge just beyond the hotel. Their families paid $500 damages, the carcass was taken to the tannery in Tan Yard Lane, the hide preserved and the fat rendered into "greese and taller," as Elmer Keach, (now three years dead at eighty-eight), still remembered being told as a child.

Since 1822 it had been known as Elephant Bridge. That is no longer its name. Not many youngsters went to Vietnam from Chepachet but one who died there was William Schanck. Now the bridge is officially named for him. Little had ever been done by the village to memorialize those who were killed or wounded in World War I and World War II. The renaming of the bridge still rankles some. So does a row over freshmen and sophomore high school essays which spoke critically of Richard Nixon.

"There is a very independent attitude here," muses Richmond Kent. "The shadow of things in Washington and the split over school politics touches us. People are angry about Elephant Bridge. And there is a nascent fear over the economy. The world seems more precarious. I hear it in the tapes. Not one man or woman expresses any regret at having been born. But things have not turned out as they expected. I told an old lady she had lived in 'a glorious and memorable time.' She smiled and said it was a matter of character. 'Most of our ills today,' she said, 'are psychosomatic.' "

Rhode Island was suffering nine percent unemployment in 1975. The figure was sixteen percent in Providence. Chepachet lies in a backwater. So does Providence. So does Rhode Island.

Big industry now is costume jewelry, leather goods and souvenirs. The Bicentennial brought a bit of a boom. But what *is* Chepachet today? People shop at the discounters in Providence. High school students move away. The pike takes a lot of the young to Connecticut. The village is squeezed by Providence suburbs and sees the condominiums coming. The people halted one big shopping center. What about the next? Warwick and Cranston are built up. Population is moving this way.

There is a nervous quality about life that has nothing in common with Hiram's day, nothing in common with the years that followed (the tape-recorded memories provide an almost seamless overlap with Hiram's journals). When people talk in Chepachet today they seem to sense that soon they will be marching to a different drum. The farms are gone. Industry is gone. To be a bedroom for Providence doesn't seem much of a role in life.

Richmond Kent shakes his head. There is one feeling that comes to him from recording the voices of the village. The people are not happy anymore. I shake my head with Kent. I sense, too, uneasiness in the village. It does not, I think, fit the sense of Hiram I am beginning to feel. I am not comfortable. Nor, I think, would Hiram be.

3

AT THREE P.M. THURSDAY, October 19, 1815, Hiram Salisbury set out for Canandaigua, N.Y., in his heavily laden wagon and at dusk arrived at Jo Joslin's, where he put up for the night. He had driven four miles, and the cost of his supper, his lodging and food for his horses came to 12 cents. The next day, Friday, was his first full day of travel. He covered thirty-six miles and stayed with his brother, John, at Stafford, Conn. It cost him 15 cents. He spent the weekend with John and on Monday, October 23, drove twenty-eight miles, passing through Springfield, crossing the Connecticut River by ferry and stopped the night at the Sign of the Heart, beyond Westfield. His expenses were 59 cents. The next night found him at Merrill's in the town of Lee, 31 miles. He ran into a severe snow squall. His costs were $1.18.

Hiram averaged twenty-five to thirty miles a day. He stopped at Albany to take "a hasty peep at the New car of Neptune which for neatness & accuracy of mechanism exceeds anything of the kind I ever saw." Past St. Anthony's Nose he encountered more snow squalls and "an almighty N.W. wind." At Little Falls a six-horse wagon "capsized" on the bridge and he had to ford the creek below. He then made a northward excursion to Sacket's Harbor, on Lake Ontario, where he inspected Ft. Tomkins "in which are Deposited vast quantities of ammunition in one stock of shot said to contain 16,000 24 lbers & Cost U.S. $50,000." He saw a long twenty-four pounder used on the Constitution in the war against Tripoli and a great frigate building in the docks, pierced for 80 to 90 guns, "truly a Lake Monster." He finally arrived at his father's place, Number 9, on Friday, November 24, after a little more than a month of travel. The trip cost him $13.94½, of which he paid 60½ cents in tolls and $1.25 for shoeing his horse. He collected debts of $18.89 on route and arrived at Number 9—$4.94½ richer than when he started.

I left Chepachet at two p.m. July 8, 1975, and in ten minutes I was across the Rhode Island line into a land of white Connecticut houses, built in Hiram's day or before, dairy farms and corn fields, great elms and maples shading the road up through Putnam. The backroad was blacktopped but Hiram would have recognized the way. The scent of 1815 lingers on the scene. I passed, as he did, through Woodstock and North Woodstock to Union and into Stafford Springs, an old Victorian town at the edge of the shade-tobacco country with its cheese-cloth nettings and long open curing barns. The drive took fifty-six minutes. Hiram's day equaled my hour.

The run through Somers and across Springfield to Westfield's deep lawns and old white houses took another hour, another of Hiram's days. Then west on Highway 20, parallel to the Mass Pike, along the deep bottom lands of the Westfield River, passing the edge of Beckett, a back road, deserted, little farming and one state forest after another. To Lee the time was fifty-five minutes. Another of Hiram's days. Now the houses grew richer. I was moving through Stockbridge music country, filled with summer people, people from New York and Boston, cars on the backroads, young men with beards, young women with long blonde ponytails, bluejeans and sandals. To Greenbush—another hour, another day for Hiram. Hiram passed through Albany and Schenectady to Van Eps Inn. I took the New York State Thruway to Amsterdam, pulled off to a motel that featured a Spanish Galleon restaurant. I was eating in the Spanish Galleon, roast ribs, fat and overcooked, when three stately ladies entered, tottering a little on heels a bit higher than they were accustomed to. They wore their best clothes. You knew these were their best clothes—long dresses, flower prints, high necks, small beaded bags. They were dignified and they were black. They thanked a young man who held the door open for them. They thanked the bartender when he brought them their bourbon-and-water. They bowed politely to the whole company when they walked out of the Spanish Galleon. As I went to my room I saw them in a cluster three doors down.

"Young man," they called. "Young man—won't you help us get this door open?"

Young man? Me? I went over. Of course, I went over. I took a look at the key. It was No. 14. They were trying to open the door to No. 7. They laughed and it was like warm sunshine spilling out of a silver pail. They went to get the correct key. Soon I heard the call: "Young man! Young man!" They still couldn't open the door. I opened it for them and we laughed together.

In the morning I met my three ladies again—and fifty other ladies and gentlemen, all black, all dressed in their best, the men in fine dark suits, perspiring a little in the humid morning, the ladies in their finery, walking easily, thanking the slow-moving waitresses, joking with the driver of their big Greyhound charter bus ("Don't you leave without us, now!"), carefully helping two elderly sisters in gray who were escorting them, off to the convention of their religious sisterhood, almost the only persons I met in the whole of the United States whom I could truly call ladies and gentlemen. I think they are the kind of people who traveled the Mohawk route in Hiram's day. Real people of flesh and blood and open hearts. Perhaps I'm wrong, but I think most travelers were real people in Hiram's day. In my own day, all across American I will meet real people, too. But also too many made of synthetic and plastic.

I drove along the Mohawk Valley—the old cities, Canajoharie, Little Falls, Herkimer, Utica, Rome and the boom cities of the Erie Canal, Syracuse and the rest. This year the canal was celebrating its one hundred and fiftieth birthday. It formally opened October 26, 1825, but Hiram could not wait. He boarded the canal boat *New Haven* of the Merchant Line ten miles west of Albany August 27, 1825, and paid one and one-half cents a mile passage—212 miles to Palmyra, N.Y., $3.18 fare and three meals for 50 cents. The trip took a bit more than four days and he got to his father's at Canandaigua on the evening of September 1, 1825.

I don't know whether the building of the Erie Canal was the most significant event in the first third of our country's existence or not. Probably it was. The populations of Rochester, Buffalo, Syracuse, Detroit and Chicago rose 300 percent in the decade. The canal switched trans-Atlantic commerce irrevocably from Boston and Philadelphia to New York. It opened the West. It cost $8,000,000 and paid its construction costs in twelve years. It made raising wheat west of the Alleghenies a profitable

When Mrs. Trollope saw Canandaigua in 1836 she thought it was one of the most beautiful villages in America. It has changed. (*Courtesy,* CANANDAIGUA DAILY MESSENGER)

business and it put New England farming on the skids. It had more to do with the opening of the West than all the gunfighters in Texas, the California gold rush or, even, I suspect, the Goulds, the Vanderbilts and the railroad barons.

I traveled along the Mohawk and the canal from Utica to Palmyra. The canal was dead. No more drums along the Mohawk. Here and there an oil barge. Here and there a cabin cruiser. The locks well oiled. The bridges ship-shape. But the villages and towns along the way a long dark stain of decay.

At Palmyra I turned south on 21, the same road Hiram took when he got off the canal boat *New Haven*. The rye was red in the fields. I saw a large sign on the left side of the road. It proclaimed: CANANDAIGUA—HISTORIC, SCENIC, PROGRESSIVE. I had come back. This was where my great-great-grandfather settled in 1802, coming from Chepachet. His wife, Mary, wrote of the trip, "toting one baby, one mirror, one pocket full of silver money and dragging one toddler"—that toddler would have been my great-grandfather Amasa. If Chepachet and the Revolutionary days were a little blurred in my vision—not so

Canandaigua. Canandaigua was precisely outlined in the letters and journals, in stories I'd heard. In fact, I knew that the old house at Number 9 still survived. I had its picture. I would seek it out.

> The little town of Canandaigua . . . is as pretty a village as ever man contrived to build. Every house is surrounded by an ample garden and at that flowery season they were half buried in roses. It is true these houses are of wood but they are so neatly painted in such perfect repair and shew so well within their leafy setting that it is impossible not to admire them.
> —*Frances Trollope, June 5, 1831 (from* DOMESTIC MANNERS OF THE AMERICANS)

Historic, Scenic, Progressive . . . I had not read Mrs. Trollope as I came upon Canandaigua on the hot July day. I followed my nose past WEZO, the stereo radio station, past a big blue water tank, past the huge Veterans Hospital, the biggest thing in town, down Main Street, past the handsome dome of the Ontario County Courthouse, slowly across the barred stripes of the Senior Citizens' Cross-Walk, on down Main Street with its red-white-and-blue trash cans, the pizza parlor, the clusters of bikers in all-black plastic and suddenly I arrive at the Strip, the head of the beautiful Canandaigua lake, which captured Mrs. Trollope's eye.

There it was—a bit of the Catskills, a rural Coney Island. Roseland Amusement Park, Caruso's Restaurant, boat rides, Italian sausages, submarines, mini-scooters, frozen custard, Sno-Kones, a merry-go-round and ferris wheel, the Skyliner Roller Coaster and the Yo-Yo, the Skee-Ball, the Gay Nineties Restaurant, The Finish-Line, The Magic Carpet, a drive-in theater showing *Flesh Gordon* and *The Groove Tube,* both X-rated, an old Federal house painted salmon pink and turned into a motel, "The Future Home of Finger Lakes College", a mobile-home park, a liquor store, Kellogg's Pan Tree Motor Inn, the Lakeside Motor Inn, the Twin Birches Motel, the Colonial Inn, Polimeni's Italian-American Restaurant, Carvel ice cream, Kentucky Fried Chicken and a Sheraton Motor Inn.

I cannot believe my eyes. Oh, I know the country has changed. I know history is being transformed into plastic souvenirs and synthetic 13-star flags made in South Korea. This is Canandaigua?

I *know* 130 years have passed since Amasa sold Number 9

and moved to Wisconsin. I know Canandaigua lives by its race-track, its Veterans Hospital, the big Mobil warehouse for plastic meat trays and plastic egg cartons (which burned a few days later). I know it lives for its colony of senior citizens. It is late afternoon and I see the senior citizens, the ladies with their too-careful makeup, their dresses which shrink from their bones, their thin, thin legs and cautious small steps ("Last week Maude fell and broke her hip. That's one thing *I'm* going to avoid"); the men, some still sporting panama hats with black bands and their heavy canes. They begin to move early, some-time before four o'clock. They move out of the rooming houses, out of the senior-citizen compounds, the nursing homes, the non-nursing homes, and cheap condominiums, the cheap flats, the massive citadel of Grove Home for Senior Citizens, a grey-stone castle of 1855, set back on an oak-shaded park, hundreds of them coming out into the open air. They begin to move from their cells, those who are able, in the late afternoon. They move down the side streets and onto Main. Only a few have the money to eat on the Strip. They cannot afford Vecchi's, Poli-meni's; the fried clams, Italian sausage and pizza upset worn digestive tracts. They file into the small cafés on Main Street, the ones with worn white curtains at the windows and the ones with neon beer signs beckoning to a dark interior. They come in for the shrimp platter, served with Irish bread, salad and a thin ice-cream desert. It costs $2.75. They can't afford that every evening. You see them gliding into the supermarkets and vari-ety stores. They pick up a no-brand chicken TV plate, a frozen no-brand hamburger or a glassine package of cheese crackers and slip back (but slowly) to their cells. They move carefully and look at the others on the street with open anger, the anger of unfulfillment, fear, poverty, emptiness. They are angry be-cause they are old and they do not know what to do with their lives and they are afraid of poverty and illness and death. They have come to Canandaigua because they have heard that it is cheaper and because they cannot afford Miami or Arizona. Some, perhaps, have come because of the races. You see these in the Italian restaurants. They are brisker than their comrades, the men in checked suits and sports jackets. The women have blondined their hair until it cracks at the touch. They do not go to the track but they talk of going. They do not buy *Racing Form* but they talk of it. They do not bet on the races but they talk of the bets they have not made. I should not exaggerate. Some actually go to the races. These are the ones who talk slyly about life in the condominiums.

John Salisbury and his sons built this house in Section 9, near Lake Canandaigua, about 1800. It was known as No. 9, the Home Place.

"It's not a place for old people, you know," one quickly says.

"We have all kinds of people. Mr. Sumerfeld talks with his office in New York every morning and Mrs. Shapiro has a real-estate business. I think she's quite active."

They hint at all kinds of things that "go on." Even wife swapping. Even group sex. Well . . .

This was not the role of those past middle age in Hiram's time. To be sure there were the infirm. Some had to be cared for at the poor farm or kept at town expense. Hiram was overseer of the poor for a while. But the aged, as Hiram catalogued in letters to his father, usually lived on the farms. They worked as they could. If they were bound up with arthritis or what they called sciatica they did little, sitting by the fire in winter, sunning themselves on the bench outside the door on warm days. But there was always something for the elderly to do—minding the baby, carding the wool, weeding the kitchen garden, sorting the beans, whittling dolls. They whittled a lot in those days.

Hiram or John or Amasa could not have imagined a society which systematically segregated able-bodied people, sequestered them in institutions (granted this is masked by Madison Avenue verbiage), condemned them to idleness, severed their normal relations with families, factories, offices and institutions, and set them down on the frayed edges of the real world, there to live out their days in frustration, venting their hostility in alcohol, golf and quarrels.

These men, the two sons and the veteran who fought with Washington and whose grave, a simple eroded slab of marble bearing his birth-and-death dates, stands in the little cemetery of Cheshire, a faded cotton flag and a tarnished metal tag with the words "Veterans Memorial" (Imagine! No word of his Revolutionary service!) could not have conceived a social system so perverse.

Nor can I.

I do not know what we think we are doing. I know that it is wrong. Very wrong. I know what society was like in the days of these three men. I know what it was like in my childhood where the family of grandparents, uncles, aunts, cousins and connections was the rule. I know it was better then. I have seen such a society preserved in China. It *is* possible to unite all the people in a common concern. We did it one hundred and fifty years in our Republic. I am angry. Not with the people I see on the sidewalks of Canandaigua. Not, to be sure, with this once-lovely New York town. I am angry with my America and my fellow Americans. We can do better than this. We will, too.

Finally I found Number 9. I wish I hadn't.

Number 9 is not a house number. It is section of land, around the corner of Lake Canandaigua on the east side, almost to Cheshire. The country is peaceful here and the land is rolling, good farming country although a neighbor, Myrtle Collins, told me: "The land is good but the farmer can't make nothing. Nobody is going into farming now." Sam Caselo, who lives a quarter-mile away owns a hundred acres or more and rents a couple of hundred. He has the old Herendeen farm, Freelove Herendeen was John's first wife, Hiram's mother. Neither Sam Caselo nor Myrtle Collins has heard of Number 9, the "Home Place" or the Salisbury farm. Down Woolhouse Road from Caselo I see an old house standing, door open, porch sagging behind a rectangle of six poplar trees. Old lilacs have grown up around the porch and a decaying barn stands behind. I get out

of the car and walk slowly into the yard and up the steps, concave with the wear of many feet, across the rotted porch. Inside
there is junk and clutter—folding chairs, a child's bed, beer
cases, wooden tables, boxes of old machinery and rusty tools.
On top of one heap a State Highway sign, stolen from some
roadside: $50 FINE FOR LITTERING. I do not want to believe it
but it is true. I know the house from the picture. I have come
home. This is Number 9.

Up the road I find Glen Benjamin, a real-estate developer.
He owns Number 9. Bought it with a partner eight years ago.
Wanted to get away from the "rat race" of Rochester and came
down to this countryside. He's built four split-levels so far on
the land, including one for himself, one for his son.

The old house? Oh, yes. It's a party house. You know, we
invite our friends over for parties and camp-outs. Folks come
and camp in the yard. They stay the night. Had a big one on
Fourth of July. Tore off the old woodshed, put it on a big pile of
brushwood and you should have seen it burn. Gosh, what a
blaze!

We go back through the house. In the rear there's a
kitchen and an old pantry, a toilet that's been put in sometime
in this century. The parlor and living-room wallpaper is very,
very old. How old I can't guess, at least a hundred years, probably more. The staircase goes up on tiny risers, just wide enough
for your toes, almost straight up. Upstairs no one has touched
the old wide floorboards. There are four bedrooms crammed
under the eves, two dormers in front. Number 9 must have
bulged in the 1820s and 1830s. All that family living there and
relatives in and out.

Benjamin's son thinks the stones holding up the porch will
go well in the new house he is hoping to build "in the old
style." Mrs. Benjamin is still digging up the "marvelous old
flowers" she's found growing around Number 9.

"You've no idea," she says. "It's such a wonderful party
house. Our friends just love to come there."

Benjamin had wanted to tear down Number 9 but couldn't
under the terms of his mortgage. His son is still eager. He wants
to use the old lumber.

"We better wait a bit," Benjamin muses. "You know if this
house gets written up it will be worth a lot."

Worth a lot . . . I don't know. It seems too late for Number
9. Perhaps it would be best that it met the end which fate seems
to be preparing. Party houses and fires go hand in hand.

Perhaps next time it will not be the shed that goes up in such a splendid blaze. As Cora Kent in Chepachet said of a man named Ruflus, who tried to burn down the stagecoach inn nearly one hundred years ago: "Oh, what a thing it is to set a fire! You don't know where it is going to stop."

Most farms are sold through the Grange or by the farmers among themselves. But Benjamin has a big demand for farmettes —everyone wants one. City people, young people. Everyone wants a piece of land and a country house. I wonder why. I wonder what they will do with their farmettes and their land and if anything lies hidden in this desire besides nostalgia. There may be something more elemental astir among the people.

A hundred years ago Canandaigua and Chepachet served an economic and social purpose. They filled a need. So did the people who lived there. They made things, grew things. Theirs was a productive economy. The mills hummed and in the farm kitchens the handicrafts survived, women carded the wool, spun it into yarn, wove it and turned it into clothing. They did it here on Woolhouse Road. Number 9 for years was a sheep farm. The Wool House was just down the road.

On this day Benjamin, his bearded son, his daughter-in-law, his wife and friends sit around a cement-floored patio. They are collecting old furniture and no longer needed household utensils for a tag sale. They are friendly people, sitting, gossiping and drinking beer. Around them are heaped the broken artifacts of a discarded way of life.

I am, I confess, shaken by Canandaigua. The Mohawk trail that I have followed has become a trail of desolation. Town after town is dying, the old people idle, the young people vanishing, the mills silent, the river forlorn, the canal unused. And now Number 9.

Around me the gentle hills lie green and yellow in the late July afternoon. The corn is being harvested. I drive back to Canandaigua, thinking of Hiram's entry for August 23, 1817: "At Seth Ross's pondering." I ponder. Why am I so disturbed? It is not just the land, so much of it turned to litter and waste. The honkey-tonk of Canandaigua. Not the houses, often the only monument a family leaves behind. It is the people. We are trashing our people. We spend our lives making plastic Coca-Cola cups or punching ciphers into electronic machines. We run beauty parlors for dogs and car-wash joints. We beer our bellies and glaze our eyes before inane TV programs, and in the end the funeral directors lay us out in synthetics, rouge our faces and turn on closed-circuit music in the viewing rooms. What have we given our country? What have we made of our lives? How are we using our land, our bodies, our minds, our precious American heritage? The waste of it all. It comes to me so keenly perhaps because of the years of my life spent in countries where they do not have abundance, they cannot afford waste. Nor could they in Hiram's day. Every hand was needed—the young, the old, even the crippled. Never had there been a society so profligate as ours. We had the machines, the electronic pushbuttons. The people? Let them enjoy their "leisure."

More than one million families in the whole Union are descended from the noble [New England] stock. They take to all the Union a manual skill that makes North America a walking arsenal of workmen with an iron-like energy. . . . They promote and preside over schools, books, elections and in the great enterprises of colonization and railroads, of banks and societies.
— *Domingo Faustino Sarmiento, 1847*

I SUPPOSE THAT I was seven years old when I first saw my great-grandfather's farm in Oregon, Wisconsin. I remember the morning—warm sunshine just beginning to filter through high elms and dew heavy in the grass along the dirt road. It was a white house with a porch, a rather prosperous-looking house, and in a field beside the house was growing a plant with leaves like velour, palish green and soft to the touch. Tobacco, my father said. My sister and I picked some of the leaves and took them back home where they stayed in the drawer of my applewood commode until, I suppose, my mother finally threw them out. They didn't smell like tobacco. In fact, they had turned black and rotted.

Amasa went to Oregon in 1846. This was the big leap. His father had died nine years before. He sold Number 9 and went west. Many of his neighbors in Canandaigua had gone before. Two brothers were already in Wisconsin. He traveled with his wife and three children (one of them my grandfather, Augustus Harrison) and a dozen relatives and friends. They were part of the migration of millions onto the new lands of the west. Every day the canalboats were jammed. Amasa's boat was so loaded his goods had to be left on deck in the rain until they reached Rochester from Palmyra. The passengers pressed up on the bridges to push the boat down low enough to pass under.

Amasa took the steamboat *Superior* to Milwaukee and hired three teams at $18 a team to take his goods and another at $16 to carry his family. The trip took two days from Milwaukee to Oregon.

On a bright October day I drove into Oregon with my son, Michael, one hundred miles from Milwaukee where he lives. Amasa's two days was two hours in Michael's gray Volkswagen across the glacial anomoly of the Kettle Morain, through fine dairy country, big cornfields and concrete and fieldstone silos standing in ranks like castle towers in Normandy. The oaks had turned bronze, the ash yellow, the maples red and the sumac purple. The countryside was spotted with cream-brick houses, cream-brick churches, cream-brick schoolhouses, Black Angus herds, Jerseys, Holsteins and Guernseys. The closer we came to Oregon the more tobacco barns, not open like those of Connecticut but closed or ventilated by narrow strips. Pheasants started along the roads and whirred over the plowed fields. We had driven into the heartland of America. I felt at home.

Heartland America . . . The old Salisbury farm is remarkably intact. True, across the street now stands the Holy Mother Consolation Catholic Church, a plaster white Jesus in a blue shrine in front, and along the flank of the old farm a developer has put in two rows of single-level houses. The floor plans are identical but each is a different color—green, salmon, gray, baby blue. They differ in another way. Outside each house is a rural mailbox mounted atop an old farm milk can. One can is painted black, one green. Another has been placed beside the front door step and filled with red geraniums. And one is spattered with decal fishes and decal flowers.

The future doesn't look promising but—the house is there, the farm is there and Harold Thompson, who has lived here all his life, ever since the farm was sold by my grandfather's brother, DeWitt Clinton, in 1913, works the land and makes a good living. He puts in crops of corn and oats and hay and he's not complaining. The Oregon land is some of the richest in the state. Amasa knew what he was doing when he came out in '46.

Maybe corn prices will go a bit higher this year but Thompson doesn't much care. His crop is in and already sold.

The Thompsons don't live in Amasa's old house. That was gone by 1910. They live with their daughter and three grandchildren in the one DeWitt built in 1869. When the daughter moved in, they decided to build a new house. They'd just bulldoze away the old house or burn it down. They called in the local contractor and he started to excavate for a new house about two hundred feet up the road.

"But then," said Mrs. Thompson, "the little six-year-old came running to me. He said 'Grandma, why do we have to go and live in another house? Why can't we just live here?'"

She realized suddenly that the child had lived in six different houses in six years. It was time he put down roots. They sent away the bulldozers and have been at it ever since, fixing up the old house.

"You'll have to excuse us," she said. "It's a mess."

She was right. The furniture was piled in corners. Stacks of linoleum stood in the dining room, rolls of synthetic walnut paneling in another. It was so hard, she said, to get workmen and so few of them were any good. All the same she thinks Oregon is a good community. True, people aren't like they were when she was growing up. The schoolteacher has to send notes home to parents telling them to spend an hour or two with their children, to show some interest in what they are doing. Mrs. Thompson is indignant that the school should have to tell mothers and fathers how to treat their children. When I was growing up, she says, it was the other way around.

Oregon is a good town to live in. Yes, prices are high. But people are getting on pretty well. The trouble is that Oregon is just a bedroom town for Madison. That's only ten miles away. There's no longer a shoemaker in Oregon. You have to go to Madison to get your shoes fixed. No clothing store, either. There used to be a bakery. Now the bread and cake comes from Stoughton, eight miles away.

"We're lucky there's a good bakery there," Mrs. Thompson says. She buys the Stoughton bread and cookies for her grandchildren. But most people buy store bread. White and bland.

"Everything's changing," she says. "But this is a good place to bring up kids in. We have the doctor across the road at the clinic and our banker lives next door."

As she talks there is a low rumble, and I see the huge paws

Amasa Salisbury went west to Wisconsin by canal boat and lake steamer in 1846. The passengers had to press up on the bridges so that the boat could sail under them.

and head of a St. Bernard rearing up to the window. He's in a wove-wire pen beside the house. Mrs. Thompson says she got him because of the children. So many people go up and down the highway. You just don't know who they are. Yes, she knows St. Bernards are supposed to be so gentle. This one is, too, with the children. But any stranger he'd tear apart.

Mrs. Thompson has one complaint. The land, better than one hundred acres of the original Salisbury one hundred twenty-nine, is taxed by the village as "development land," not farming land. It's the last farm in Oregon and it's as though the town just didn't want anyone to farm anymore. Of course, the Thompsons want to go on farming—but who can say?

This rich Wisconsin soil became the domain not only of the Salisburys and Deans and Eatons and Pratts and all the others who went west from Chepachet and Canandaigua but of thousands of New Englanders from Massachusetts and Maine and New Hampshire. Often they moved as Amasa did, on a second leg, having farmed some years in upstate New York. They came because the land was better. Because the land was cheap. Because they could sell higher in the new markets opened up by the waterways and the railroads. New England provided the foundation. On it was soon to be erected the structure of German, Scandinavian and later Polish and east European emigration which today gives Wisconsin its ethnic, cultural and social shape.

I never knew my great-grandfather, Amasa. He died long before I was born. But he is the first of the tribe whom I would recognize. He had his portrait painted, and old daguerreotypes survive of himself and his wife, Sarah. He was carved out of the classic stone of New England, high cheekbones, side whiskers, eyes (they were blue) that peer out from overhung brows, a stern man, a calvinistic-looking man (I don't believe he was a calvinist at all), a strong man. He supported the schools and the libraries. He was prosperous but not too prosperous. He worked his Wisconsin farm all his life. He put his boys, my grandfather, Harrison, and his brother, DeWitt, through the local academy and the University of Wisconsin. He and Sarah drove their wagon to Madison, taking apples and potatoes for the boys to live on. Sometimes, that was all they had. Once Sarah baked six pies, which Harrison and his roommates devoured in two days. The roads were so bad in winter, horses went almost up to their bellies in mud. The boys walked from Madison to Oregon and back. DeWitt got lost in a blizzard and wandered around until morning. For a while Harrison lived in a room so far from the campus he walked six miles a day back and forth to his classes.

The war—the Civil War—came up like thunder in the Wisconsin heartland. This was Lincoln country, and as DeWitt recorded in his diary April 20, 1861, Wisconsin was asked for 790 volunteers in the first call. "They can be had and thousands more if needed," he added a bit sententiously. But Amasa was not eager to lose his boys. Enthusiasm for the war was one thing. Fighting in it was another.

It was not until 1864 with the war well on the way to Union victory that Harrison and his senior Wisconsin class were carried away by enthusiasm. The class, en masse, enlisted, thirty recruits, all, as Harrison said, "but copperheads and cripples." The class signed up May 12, 1864, for one hundred days. Harrison spent his service guarding stores at Memphis. He fired no bullets, none were fired at him. But he learned a lesson more important than firing a gun. He met a freed Negro working in a field, "a spelling book in one hand and his hoe in another."

"This ought to be a lesson to us who, having every opportunity to improve our minds, waste our time," he wrote. "I think Negroes can teach us something after all."

On June 22, which would have been Commencement Day had his class remained at Madison, he and his friends visited a Negro regiment. The blacks had the neatest, most comfortable camp he had seen.

"It is said," he wrote, "that at the late battle at Gin Town they fought with the greatest bravery even after the officers had deserted them."

The lesson was one that stayed with Harrison. He had never met a black before he joined the Union Army.

By 1868 Harrison had his medical degree from Ann Arbor, had completed his internship at Bellevue and gone back to marry Mary Pritchard at Mazomanie, Wisconsin, and set up medical practice there. DeWitt married, too, and took over the family farm. This generation was in the heartland to stay. Here and there one would join the next migratory wave to the Pacific Coast, but for the most part the great trek had ended here in this fertile land with its steady succession of seasons, the cold winters, the long uncertain springs, the hot summers and the glorious autumns. This was the human stock which would build Middle America; which would make "the most magnificent habitation ever prepared by God for man" its dwelling place. These were the people and this was the land that nurtured me.

Michael and I drove on to Mazomanie, skirting Madison. Here my grandfather treated his first patients, here my father was born in 1869 in a little red-brick house a block from the millpond where he nearly drowned. Here my grandmother and a gay group of girls went hop-picking in the summer and picnicking on School Section bluff. Here Old Unk, the gentlest, least commercial of men, had gone into the fanning-mill business and failed.

Mazomanie . . . heart of the heartland.

The Oyster and The Eagle

When God made the Oyster he granted him absolute economic and social security. He built the Oyster a House, his shell, to protect him from his enemies. When Hungry the Oyster simply opens his shell and food rushes in for him. He has Freedom from Want.

But when God made the Eagle he declared: "The Blue sky is the limit. Build your own Home there." So the Eagle went on the highest Mountain. Storms threaten every day. For Food he flies through miles of Rain and Snow and Wind.

The Eagle not the Oyster is the Emblem of America.

—*Yellowed typescript pasted to the cash register of the Village Life Cafe, Mazomanie. (The waitress said she never noticed it there.)*

They're putting in a new sewer, paving and curbing in front of the house where my father was born. Big lilacs block the front door and Michael and I go around to the back where a knock on the broken screen brings a blond seventeen-year-old and her stocky aproned mother to the door. The mother is Thankful Coopernall and the girl is her second daughter, Christy, who has never been out of the state of Wisconsin. Five generations of women have been called Thankful, but Mrs. Coppernall's granddaughter has been named Heidi Thankful "because it's so confusing on the telephone. You always have to say: Which Thankful, the older or the younger?" "My name," the seventeen-year-old says, "was going to be Patience Serene. But my mother changed her mind and I'm Christy Christine."

I can't describe the Mazomanie house. When Thankful moved in seventeen years ago she hated the brown wallpaper with its big heraldic designs. She told the children to paste up anything they wanted and they have—posters, cut-out ads, magazine covers, crayon scribbles. On all sides are stacked

*Werner Thiers, blacksmith and historian of Mazomanie, Wisconsin.
No reason, he believes, why small towns should die if they serve
people. (Courtesy,* IAN PATRICK)

jumbles of things—pottery, small glass dishes, a 1940s Zenith
radio, Haviland china that belonged to Thankful's mother, old
pewter, dolls, magazines, books, papers, beautiful old kerosine
lamps. "You should have come on Sunday," Thankful says.
"Then we would be all cleaned up." I wonder.

I tell Thankful I'm interested in history. She gasps: "I'm a historian!" She's just gotten her degree at the University of Wisconsin, a major in journalism, a minor in history.

"At your age why did you go to college?" I ask.

"I don't like welfare," she snaps. She is a licensed practical nurse. When she was injured in an accident, national rehabilitation paid for her college course.

Mazomanie, she says, is a great town for history. She directs me to Werner Thiers. ("He's the blacksmith. He knows all about it.") He does. Werner Thiers is not only a blacksmith he is a local historian, a real one, a founder of the Mazomanie Historical Society, founder and director of the Mazomanie Historical Museum, a tall, graying man, strong as you'd expect a blacksmith to be. This afternoon he's come down to work in the Museum with his five-year-old grandson for company. He came to Mazomanie more than thirty years ago and bought the blacksmith shop. "The shop has had only two owners since 1900 and I'm one."

"I've been to Europe," Werner reflects. "I've seen the museums there. They are palaces. They have all the riches of the emperors and kings. But the common things are gone. The museums are magnificent but there's not much to show how common people live."

The Mazomanie museum is dedicated to common people. One whole white-painted wall of the old stone mill that houses it is given up to the farm tools that made Mazomanie, ordinary iron implements, passed down generation by generation.

"History books write up wars and politics," Werner says. "But history is made everywhere. Here in Mazomanie and in the other small towns of America. That's what our museum is about. About our life here in this small town and this countryside."

He has a theory about museums. There was one in McGregor, Iowa, where he grew up. When people know and preserve their history they know and preserve their pride.

"If you'd come to this town thirty years ago," he says, "and saw how run down things were you'd hardly imagine it today. Today we have community spirit."

Werner knows what Mazomanie was like when young Dr. Augustus Harrison Salisbury set up practice here. It was a bustling place, a town built by English land speculation, the British Temperance Emigration Society of Liverpool, England, which brought nine hundred people in, my grandmother's mother among them, and a railroad speculation, the Milwaukee and Mississippi (Amasa mortgaged seventy acres of good land to buy M & M stock and regretted it the rest of his life).

Harrison came to Mazomanie, of course, because this was where his wife, Mary, lived with her family and her friends.

But there were other good reasons. Mazomanie bubbled with life. There was still hope that it might become *the* center of Wisconsin rather than Madison. In fact, the lots where Harrison's house was built had been bought by Governor Chadbourne Washburn purely as a land speculation.

When Werner Thiers moved to Mazomanie, people kept dropping into his blacksmith shop and asking if he knew that next door was the shop where John Preston had made John Appleby's "knotter." Werner had never heard of the knotter. Now he thinks it was one of the most significant inventions of nineteenth-century America, a simple iron ratchet which automatically tied baling knots. The Appleby knotter made it possible to bind wheat and bale hay. Essentially the same simple Appleby device is used in modern balers.

"You know," Werner adds, "the knotter was one of the ten most important inventions of the nineteenth century."

Perhaps it was, perhaps it wasn't. But it was valuable in opening up the heartland. And it was characteristic of that ingenuity which caused Grund to conclude that the Yankees were responsible for "most of the valuable improvements of the century."

Mazomanie was a Yankee town. When Harrison opened his practice, the village and township had a population of 1700 (today it is 1376). The biggest enterprise was the N. T. Davies (he was a cousin of Mary's) factory. Davies made fanning mills, simple wooden contraptions that separated seed from chaff.

He produced the Mazomanie Wagon, a practical farm wagon sold by Shower and Walter, and the Darlington washer, a home washing board, and a curious table game invented and sold by the Stark Manufacturing Company, involving three billiards on the green felt surface of a concave table. The table was fitted with a folding lid and could be used for cards, dominoes or checkers. (Werner has one in the museum). Mazomanie had a brewery, started in 1851, which produced Imperial Export Beer and consumed the local hops which Mary and her friends picked, a knitting factory, a flour mill and a company that sold organs and sewing machines, carting them around the countryside on a flatbed wagon and selling them to farmers. The railroad built a roundhouse, kept two engines in Mazomanie (one was named for the town in 1858), and over the years Mazomanie turned out "hundreds of railroad men." Mazomanie by a small stretch of Chippewa dialect on the part of the Milwaukee and Mississippi superintendent, Edward Brodhead, means "Walking Iron" or "The Iron That Walks." When Harrison started practice the town had four undertakers, three dentists and three other doctors, including W. H. Tamling, "Magnetic Physician. Will cure all curable diseases by laying on of the hands."

But if Mazomanie bustled—other towns bustled even more. Minneapolis, three hundred miles north, was doubling its population every five years. It was said to be the fastest-growing city in the country. Perhaps, that would be a better location for an energetic young doctor. Harrison left his wife and little son, Percy, in Mazomanie and went to Minneapolis, to the worry of Mary who did not relish her dark and handsome husband living in a boarding house, meeting the beautiful young ladies of Minneapolis, writing articles in the newspapers, going out to dinner every night, making a splash in order to become known and lay the foundation for his practice. As soon as she could, she packed up and followed him. Harrison had mortgaged his span of horses, carriage, harness, cutter and buffalo robe for $306 and his stock of drugs for $410 to finance the move. He sold the little red-brick house and cast his fate with the lumber-and-flour milling town of Minneapolis, entering partnership with a fellow New Englander, A. E. Ames (whose son "Doc Ames," won notoriety at the pen of Lincoln Steffens as the crookedest city politician he had ever encountered), establishing offices on the second floor corner of the new Masonic Temple building, a grandiose imagination in hewn red Minnesota sandstone and built a gothic red-painted, green-trimmed Victorian house under curving elms at 107 Royalston Avenue, where I grew up and where my heart still lies.

What happened to Mazomanie? I am standing in the October sunshine beside the orchard at Verne Lawler's house. Werner's grandson is piling red and purpled windfalls in a wheelbarrow. Up on School Section bluff I see the outlines of the great star which blazes crystal white over Mazomanie at Christmas time. For years Lawler worked as a steamfitter in Madison, driving back and forth each day. Now he helps Werner in the Mazomanie Museum.

Werner answers. He has thought a lot about this question. The towns and villages in Wisconsin were laid out for the convenience of the farmers. The farmers had to get up early, do their chores, hitch up, go to town, do their shopping and get back by noon. Well, that meant the town couldn't be more than four or five miles away. But now, the farmer can step into his pickup and be in Madison quicker than he used to drive to Mazomanie. Now the towns are in terrible competition. It's a fight for survival.

"You have to remember something about these towns," Lawler observes. "The people who built them were more crazy to make money those days than we are now. It was all speculation. If the railroad came through, they were sure they'd make a fortune."

True, Werner agrees. But even so the people worked together. It took a plow and eight oxen to break the prairies. There were not many plows, and a man would lend his to his neighbors. They worked together to break the prairie.

Still I cannot imagine what happened to all the factories, all the businesses, all that Yankee ingenuity.

Changes came, Werner says. The factories were small. They made quality articles in small quantities. A lot of handicraft went into the product. Perhaps the small factories weren't too efficient, and there wasn't capital for them to grow bigger. One by one they failed.

"By 1900," Werner says, "they were all gone. Every single one of them."

There were attempts to move in other directions. The museum has preserved the main curtain of the Schmitz Opera House. Ringling Brothers came over from Baraboo and put on their first circus performance at the Opera House. Schmitz ordinarily charged $12 for the use of the house. But the circus drew only $17 at the box office so he cut the charge to $8. (Schmitz lent old Unk $75 on April 21, 1872, on collateral of a mare and eight fanning mills. It didn't save Unk's business from going under.)

The Opera Curtain carries an advertisement for Mazomanie's newest venture:

Mazomanie is rapidly becoming a famous poultry center.
Push Poultry Raising. There is Big Money in it.
Mazomanie Poultry and Egg Co.

Well, there wasn't that "Big Money." Gradually the town entered a period of decline and drift.

What of it now?

Lawler answers. The young people move away. They grow up and move away. They say of Mazomanie: "Such a town! Such a town!" But later many of them move back. It looks better then. It's a very friendly town. You know how people are in a small town.

"Yes," says Werner carefully. "You can be a big cog in the wheel in a town like Mazomanie. You should see how people pitch in for our Wild West days. Everybody gets into it."

But what, I wonder, can you do in a town like this. People live here and work in Madison. Is there any place to work in Mazomanie? They smile. Lawler takes me out along the railroad tracks and points up the line a quarter-mile or so. There sprawls an industrial plant, a spread of characteristically low, single-story hatches. It gleams blue and aluminum in the afternoon sun.

"That's the Wicks plant," Lawler says. "It stands where the hop yard was that your grandmother picked hops in."

This is Wick Building Systems, a producer of prefab houses and prefab farm buildings. It has grown from nothing in 1956 when Wick came to Mazomanie and started into business in the garage back of his house to an enterprise which employs more than seven hundred men and women.

This, I say, looks like what was happening in Mazomanie one hundred years ago—a combination of native ingenuity, aggressiveness and local opportunity.

Werner's eyes twinkle.

No reason, he thinks, why small towns should die so long as they serve a useful purpose. Towns are made for people. If they serve the people—they will live. If they do not—why should they live? Serve the people. It's a phrase I know well. It was engraved in Chinese characters against a red enamel background on the small badges I saw Premier Chou En-lai and the other Chinese leaders wearing in 1972. It is, in fact, a quotation from Chairman Mao Tse-tung.

America marks the highest level, not only of material well-being but of intelligence and happiness which the race has yet attained—[this] will be the judgment of those who look not at the favored few for whose benefit the world seems hitherto to have framed its institutions but at the whole body of the people.

—*James Bryce, 1888*

I wonder, I wonder how much sense this all makes. Is there a social structure here in the heartland flexible enough, sturdy enough, to bridge the past and present, to build a way to the future? In the evening we talk—my son, Mike, his wife, Molly, a group of their friends, young married people, upwardly mobiles in the awkward phrase of Madison Avenue. They are in law and business, banks and finance. One young woman is a reporter. Another runs an art gallery. They live in Milwaukee's Downer Street area, a local reflection of Greenwich Village.

One of the women speaks. Her husband is a securities analyst. I like old houses, she says. I loved my grandmother's house. It smelled of old wood and of life. I don't like new houses and new apartments. That's why we live in this neighborhood. The new houses are all metal doors and plastic. I like wood and real plaster and lathes. Wallboard is no good. Old things are better. Her talk reminds me of the house where I grew up. There was a different smell to each room, real smells, not the viscous smell of plastic, the homogenized smell of to-day's detergents.

I tell them a story Lawler told me of a farmer who rented out a house next to his own. One day he noticed that his tenants were gone. Vanished. Hadn't paid their rent. They'd left their furniture behind. He asked his lawyer if he could seize their things for the rent. The lawyer thought this was too compli-cated. Why not burn the house down? It was just an old place. Then he would have an excuse to take the furniture out. So the farmer did just that—called in the local fire department, carted out the furniture and burned the house down.

One of Mike's friends chimes in. He knew an antique dealer who had hoped to get some old furniture from his uncle who lived in southern Indiana. No luck. The uncle took the old furniture, put it in an old barn and burned it up.

There's a real thing in this country for destruction, said the girl who likes old things. I have my grandmother's old china. It feels so good in your hands. But no one else in the family wanted it. They wanted to smash it. I had to argue with them to give it to me.

Yes, I thought. The passion to destroy, to eradicate the old. It's not enough to abandon an old house. It must be burned. The old furniture with it and the old china, too. What can moti-vate these people? Guilt? Do they want to destroy the evidence of their treason to the old way of life?

But destruction is not the philosophy of these young

people. They like old wooden bowls and spoons, iron beds, brass beds, old wooden school desks, anything made by hand. Molly makes her own rattan seat for a bentwood chair. They paint 1910 apartments white or scrape down to the old wood.

All work for large corporations but (like Mike) dream of working for themselves. Using their hands. I remember the first time Stephan saw a potter at work. He was awed. ("If I could only live and use my hands like that!") They did not know how to use their hands. But they want to learn.

"Everyone wants to live in the country now," Molly says. "Kids want to live in the country in peace and spend their time learning and reading."

It's true, says my old friend Arville Schaleben, for many years managing editor of *The Milwaukee Journal*. He is teaching at Madison and at Indiana and Northwestern. He sees young people every day. They are thinking of settling in Watertown and Stevens Point. They want to *count*. They are disillusioned about the Big Press—in spite of Woodward and Bernstein. They want to go to Richland Center and make a life for themselves.

What about the system, do they still expect something from it? Some think that when their turn comes, they can make the system work as they want it to work and bring back the values of the past, the ethic of New England, the spirit of the Pioneer, the community of the Heartland.

But Molly thinks the young are not sure any longer that their day will come.

One thing is certain, Arv notes, the young people don't give a damn about growth, and there they stand 180 degrees away from their grandfathers. They don't care if Wisconsin never gets another resident from out of the state. They believe in wilderness and conservation and pure air and water. They are looking for permanence in a transitory world. They worship the artifacts which Werner has so carefully assembled in the Mazomanie Museum. They are skeptical on questions of socialism, radical conservatism, any organized system of political thought. The present system doesn't work, but they have no reason to believe others would work better. They are individualists. They detest cant. None have children, but if and when they do they will have children because they want them, *want* them to live with, want them to love. They resent friends who have children and then complain about how terrible they are, how they won't mind, how they interfere with their lives and keep them from going out. "They shouldn't be permitted to have children," says a girl. A young man says: "They're so crazy. Children make the best pets."

There's a feeling of courtesy and consideration about the young people Arv sees. They are kind to each other and polite.

They've mellowed, Molly thinks. The Sixties were a very frantic time.

Who do the young people blame for the way the world is today, I ask.

Arv smiles the dry smile he has smiled since the days when we worked together on *The Minnesota Daily*, the campus paper, in the 1920s.

"Well," he says slowly, "the young people blame people like you and me. And that really mows you down."

5

Minneapolis (700–800 ft. above the sea), the largest city in Minnesota and the chief flourmaking place in the world. . . . The population in 1890 was 164,738, including many Scandinavians. Minneapolis owes its prosperity and rapid growth to the extensive and fertile agricultural district tributary to it, and to the splendid waterpower of the St. Anthony Falls. . . . In 1870 the population was 18,000, and in 1880 it was 46,000; while the last decade showed an increase of 252 percent.

—*Baedecker's* UNITED STATES, *1893*.

I HAVE NOT LIVED in Minneapolis for forty-five years, but I think there has hardly been a day of my life that I did not think of it. I have closed my eyes at night in a Siberian hotel and walked through each room of our old house at 107 Royalston Avenue and looked at each picture on the wall, each rug on the floor, and each person as they sat and talked there. I have waited for Christmas outside the double doors of the parlor and sat at the big table for Thanksgiving. I have seen Mr. Sharpless firing up his Stanley Steamer across the street and hoped once again he'd offer to take me on a ride. At such times it seemed to me that I had never left home.

In June of 1975 I went back to Minneapolis for the fiftieth reunion of my class at North Side High School. I drove my sister Janet's car down town, parked it on Seventh Street and began a walk I have walked a thousand times. Particularly, I remember the walk on winter nights, hurrying past the brooding Butler Brothers warehouse, past the dark loading ports and onto the iron-fretted bridge across the Great Northern tracks, the wooden walkway worn and splintered and the hot funnel of a locomotive just below blasting up clouds of steam and soot-grained smoke; across the bridge as fast as a small boy's feet could carry me, running down the far side and past the Pittsburgh coal yards, the wind blowing, the wooden gates of the coal yards bolted shut, the black dust ground into the ice, around the slow curve of Royalston Avenue and on to 107 set back on its broad lawn, all white snow, windows golden in the dusk, banging into the steamy kitchen, supper waiting on the old coal-and-gas range.

Oh, yes. I remember every crack in the bridge, every crack in the sidewalk, every frightening shadow. Now I walk past the Butler Brothers warehouse again. It stands dark and red and still threatening. And the bridge, iron girders gone, all concrete, then down Holden Street into nowhere. Nowhere. There is not a stick, not a stone, not a tree, not a house, not a street. Nothing. Acres of concrete, unilevel factories, warehouses, blacktop access roads and four-lanes. Gone 107, gone the little triangle of green opposite the house, gone the elms, gone Rappaports grocery store, gone the tailor shop, the notions store, the streets—Sixth Avenue, Royalston, Highland. Gone the memory of the streets and the houses. Gone as in a dream that was never dreamt.

A careful detective can find a clue or two. A break in a curb line. A small patch of red-brick paving still gleaming as it did on dew-washed mornings when I ran out of doors, the sun tinting the bricks with rose. The old house, I calculate, must have stood somewhere between the neat industrial boxes housing the Gopher News Company, and the Northwest Linen Services.

Sixth Avenue. That was our shopping street—Rappaports, its windows etched with half an inch of frost, the light dim, the air filled with the smell of bananas hanging in the window and pickles in the great pickle jar, swimming like pike in a salty pool. Now there is a four-lane freeway and the Orthodox synagogue where on high holy days I went from Sumner school to earn a dollar writing down the pledges has become a field of wild mustard.

At the far end of the street had stood the livery stables, smelling of harness and horses, and the firehouse my mother's father built from which three-horse teams plunged out as I

107 Royalston Avenue, Minneapolis: the house my grandfather built with pride and careful calculation, the house I grew up in and remember.

I have not lived in Minneapolis for forty-five years, but I think there has hardly been a day of my life when I did not think of it and the old house.

Royalston Avenue today. The house I grew up in is gone. Not only the house—the neighborhood, the school. The people are gone.

watched in terror, the steamer swaying behind, all sparks and smoke.

It was all gone. Not only the house, the neighborhood, the school. The people were gone. Only my sister and I survived of the company that thronged in and out of 107 Royalston in the years after Augustus Harrison built his house in pride and careful calculation, each room in a different wood; white pine for the parlor, red cherry for the living room, ash for the hall with its staircase and oak for the dining room. Tiled fireplaces in five of the rooms and an attic where I was certain magic vanishing powder and a secret staircase to China must be hidden in the cubbyholes.

Whatever else I knew I knew that this physical world was past. It had no existence but in my mind so savagely had we obliterated our physical past. But what of the children with whom I went to school? They were alive, many of them. I would see them this night at the class reunion. In their persons as in mine something of these distant days must survive. Perhaps in them I would find some reflection of myself.

The Ambassador Resort Motor Hotel stands outside the city limits of Minneapolis on the way to Lake Minnetonka where we spent our summers in the "old Moore place," a log cabin chinked with moss, when I was a child.

There is nothing to distinguish the Ambassador Resort Motor Hotel from a thousand others except perhaps its advertising. It calls itself the Island in the Sun and boasts of controlling the weather. People of the city and suburbs come here to spend weekends beside a bubble-topped swimming pool where they can drink as the kiddies splash.

Here the survivors of North Side High's Class of 1925 assemble for their class reunion. They all seem gray. Practically no one has plain white hair. We gather under the glass bubble for a drink and try to search each other out behind the fatty jowls, the wrinkles, the sagging figures that have obliterated the skinny youngsters who used to run two miles to school and two miles back to condition themselves for track. Or just for the fun of it.

It is a warm soft night but in the "controlled weather" of the Island in the Sun we swelter. The polyester collars of the men's sports shirts wilt and the class beauties, disguised within their upholstered flesh, wipe the sweat from their brows as they gulp their bourbon-and-water. We move to the "function room" for dinner. There are 250 of a class of 435 present, and I am amazed that there are not a dozen whom I recognize. I look for the one member of my Sumner school first-grade class who is here. I had come home after the first day in school and told my mother there were six Sullivans in my class. She was mildly skeptical and she was right. There were six Solomons and this was one of them. I remembered him as a tiny youngster, smallest in the class, dour, thin, brilliant. When the teacher asked us what song we wished to sing (World War I was on) he didn't ask for "Over There." His sad request was always the same: "The Worst Is Yet to Come." He had become a solid good-looking man in a double-knit suit with an easy smile and a sense of humor, a lawyer and a very successful one. I wasn't surprised. Solomon Wasserman had been the smartest boy I knew.

The alumni of North Side High School's Class of 1925 gather for their 50th anniversary reunion beside a bubble-topped swimming pool. (Courtesy, RUDOLPH JANU)

It is an easy crowd, a pleasant assemblage of people. Most of them have lived their lives in Minneapolis, but there is a fringe from retirement country, Florida, California, Arizona. They have a settled look, prosperous but not rich, pleased with their lives, their families, their city. The people on the platform are friends of mine. They had been the leaders in Class in 1925. Dr. Reuben Berman shows slides of Rudy Vallee, Sacco and Vanzetti, Al Capone, the Charleston and Fred and Adele Astaire, icons of our day. Mel Frank, class president is toastmaster. He's a Congregational minister and he tells some ministers' stories. One about holy water for pope-sicles. I can hear him telling them to the men's club meetings. He wears a blue-and-white beach shirt, his wife, Linnea, a mumu. They have a winter parish in Hawaii. The evening passes swiftly. I talk a bit, trying to compare 1925 with 1975 and look ahead at the future. I am optimistic—as usual. As we break up Mel warns us not to take the purple, brown, blue, and yellow plastic flowers from the tables. They have been lent by a classmate who is making it big in the plastic flowers line.

You couldn't say we thrilled each other. You couldn't say: Here is where America has been and look how gloriously she advances to the future. But what did I expect from the fifty-year survivors of a high school, which like everything else, had been torn down, bulldozed away to make place for a grim new fortress school of heavy concrete? After all this is heartland America—overweight, satisfied, successful, pleasant, ready to put its shoulder to the wheel but idling along tonight (and much of the time, I'm afraid) not challenged, seldom called upon, a bit lonely and even sad. Perhaps, I'd better talk to my own friends, the children of the heartland I best know.

We sit around the Flemish oak dining-room table in my sister's house, the house we moved into when 107 Royalston was sold, seven of us from North Side High and my sister, Janet, my wife, Charlotte, and husbands of two of the girls. We seven spent every afternoon together, working on *Polaris,* the school paper, writing, dreaming, arguing, squabbling, a contentious lot but what we contended over not one of us now could say.

This evening on a warm June fifty years later we sit down to try to understand who we were in 1925, who we have become in half a century, one quarter of our country's life, and where we think we are headed.

Mel Frank speaks first. He has always been the leader. He was, he says, a very poor kid. His father died in 1920.

His mother took the little insurance money and bought a grocery store at the corner of Irving and Plymouth. She soon lost all her money.

He went to Grant School. It was the toughest school in town, tougher than Sumner, where I went. It was nothing to get propositioned by eighth-grade girls. There were only two kids in the whole class who didn't carry condoms. Mel and another athlete. It wasn't that he was so pure. He was just too ignorant.

What made the difference, the reason why he came out okay and other kids not, was his mother.

It was her and it was the Fremont Avenue Church. This was a liberal Congregational church and it brought New England culture to the young people. Mrs. Faribault at the church was a very strong influence. She took a particular interest in Mel because the family was so poor. She inspired him to think of the big world.

Listening to Mel took me back to the years of World War I. I wondered what the others had done in those days. My sister and I made up Red Cross kits in little khaki containers for "the boys." We knitted mittens and handwarmers. I hated to think of the poor doughboys who received them.

Reuben Berman smiled. He is a prominent doctor with fuzzy hair and looks like a koala bear.

He sold Liberty bonds, he said. He gave two-minute speeches for Liberty bonds. All over town. And he knitted.

"We all knitted," he said. "We all knitted those little olive-green squares. God knows what became of them."

Linnea Peterson spoke. She had been editor of *The Polaris*. She and Mel became engaged when they were still at North Side High. She has a quiet face.

We had to write poetry at Willard school, she said, war poems. Kill the Kaiser!

"Imagine in a school named for Emma Willard," Mel said. "They had to write poems about killing the Kaiser."

Reuben went on. There had been a German doctor down in New Ulm. During the war the State Medical Society recommended to the county society that they throw him out. But the county refused. That was good.

It *was* good, I thought. The German conductor of the Minneapolis Symphony Orchestra had been thrown out in those days. Congressman Lindbergh, Charles Lindbergh's father, had been rotten-egged and ridden out of Minnesota towns for opposing the war. What chauvinists we had all been—myself included.

My sister, Janet, commented tartly: "Probably there was a large German population in New Ulm. That's why the doctor was kept."

There was a German-American bank at the corner of Plymouth and Western, Reuben recalled. It changed its name to the North American bank. For years he used to pass by and see the old name shining through where it had been painted over. German-language classes weren't restored at North High until 1922.

Alice Gates smiled. Her father was assistant principal at North in our days.

"When German classes were suspended," she said, "Miss Koenig was kept on and taught other subjects. In 1922 she went back to German."

The editors of the 1925 Polaris ~~sit around~~ the dining room table and conclude that the "Minnesota spirit" is alive and real. (Courtesy, RUDOLPH JANU)

I wondered about politics. I had been a violent partisan of Teddy Roosevelt and a violent opponent of "that yellow dog," Woodrow Wilson. I am ashamed to remember that I wore a Warren G. Harding button.

Mel peddled election handbills for all the candidates from

Lyndale to Washington Avenue and from Sixth Avenue North to Camden Place. That covered several square miles. It took some doing. He remembered being attracted to Tom Schall, the blind Congressman who went after the mining companies in northern Minnesota and said they ought to pay their fair share of taxes.

I asked Linnea whether she was a Democrat or a Republican.

"Neither! I was Swedish!" she said.

Reuben began to talk about morals. He recalled the Character Club at North High. Frank Gannon ran it. He put Reuben through a long inquisition. He asked if he masturbated. Reuben thought: This SOB. What right does he have to ask me this question. Ask me a damn fool question and you get a damn fool answer. He gave him one. He said he didn't. What bothered him was that the American people tend to be so moralistic. Their character is spotless. It is the other people who aren't so moral.

"That is part of our idealism," Linnea said.

"And our religiosity," added Mel.

We got to talking about economic differences and whether we were aware that some people were richer or poorer than others.

Mel thought we were aware of the disparity but didn't resent it. When there was a weiner roast, he always went in someone else's car. They were nice cars. He enjoyed it.

Martha Christianson Simonsen laughed. She ran the editorial page of *The Polaris*. Her face was as sweet as in 1925 and she spoke with a smile: "We rode in Harold Kaplan's blue Buick."

I wondered if we ever thought of social or class distinction—the kind of thing I'd spent half my life hearing about in Communist countries. No one thought so.

Not at all, Mel agreed. He went to work a week after his father died. He didn't tell the truth. He said he was fourteen. That was the age when you got your working papers. He got out of school at 1:30 in the afternoon and worked in a printing plant. But he didn't think that made him different from anyone else.

Mel's father had worked for the street-car company. He was involved in the big strike of 1918. He was basically with the union but he didn't walk out.

I remembered that strike. My father was in the Home Guard. He carried a big ax handle and helped break it.

Linnea's father had died in 1915. She always felt that to be

Swedish was something bad. Everyone at the top was from New England. She remembered asking Martha once: "Do you think I have a Scandinavian accent?"

Martha's father was Danish and her mother came from a New England family. Her father was a railroad contractor and he thought union men were troublemakers. He said IWW meant I Won't Work.

Mae Rockne Cruys' father and mother were divided in politics, her mother was Swedish, her father Norwegian. She was Republican, he was a Democrat. She had to be the opposite of her husband.

Alice's father was English and her mother Irish. It was a very protected home. Her father was a Republican until FDR came along. Her mother had died a Republican last year at the age of one hundred. In her family they were for the League of Nations because it was a hope for world peace. But the Senate rejected it.

"The League was a dirty word to some," Mel agreed.

Reuben's family were Jewish people who had left Russia in the 1880s and the 1890s. His father and mother both spoke Russian and Yiddish but never to the children. They had to be one hundred percent American.

What kind of a world, I wondered, had we thought we were living in—were there any doubts? I'd had none, I knew.

Reuben remembered thinking we were living in the best of all possible worlds. The idea of change never crossed his mind.

"They were great days," Mae said. "I remember when radio came in after the war. It was like a miracle. I thought it was the best of worlds. I accepted my parents' ideas. They could do no wrong."

"I thought it was a great world," Martha agreed. "Of course, I was very idealistic and naive."

But why had Minnesota been so different? I came back to my basic question—was there really a Minnesota spirit?

It had been a seedbed for honest politics, Reuben thought. There was no tremendous graft. Not even in business. And we had all been deeply influenced by religion.

Mae felt that the values of our parents had been passed on to the children. A high-school education was important. It cost quite a lot to buy books. And none of us had an idea of changing the world. It was perfect.

"There's another thing about the Scandinavian family,"

irst Row—D. Hansen, H. Salisbury, P. MacDonald, T. Parker, R. Matson, R. Berman,
econd Row—M. Wardell, O. Setzler, F. Krieg, Miss Lane, H. Reinking, M. Christensen,
hird Row—A. Feinberg, J. Erickson, M. Frank, L. Peterson, G. Mackenzie, N. Hill, R. Este

These are the editors of The Polaris *at North Side High fifty years
ago when I was a member of the Class of 1925.*

Mel added. "It was not a teetotaling society. But I can recall my
father being intoxicated only once. Every Saturday night we sat
around the table with crackers and cheese and a jug of beer."

The only time Alice could recall drinking was when some
Jewish friends gave her family some wine.

"When people came to the house mother would offer them
fruitcake and wine," Mae said. "It was the old custom."

Martha's father had been an alcoholic. She had nothing but
bad memories of drinking. Prohibition had no effect. Her father
took the Keeley cure but it didn't help.

Mae smiled sadly. Her stepfather was an alcoholic, too.
And Linnea's uncle was.

"And my father and mother were," Charlotte added.

Reuben felt that a Jewish drunk was a rarity, maybe because of the permissive attitude. Jewish families made their
own wine. Whiskey was reserved for Saturday night after services. Then each would have herring and a drink of whiskey.

I remembered my own youth. My mother had been a violent prohibitionist, a Methodist "white ribboner," a Temperance advocate. My father enjoyed a glass of wine, a bottle of beer or a drink of whiskey. There had been some violent arguments, and once mother threatened to smash all the bottles of home brew my dad had painstakingly made.

We got to talking about the school paper, *The Polaris Weekly* and what it had done for us.

Reuben thought the little weekly had set off quite a spark. He never lost his interest in writing even when he got into medical school.

"Something about it," Mae said, "was that we all worked together. Maybe that was the important thing."

"And," Alice added, "we all used our experience in some way or another."

The most important thing in his childhood, Mel believed, was that his mother introduced him to books.

"We always had books," Alice remembered. "I got dozens from the library and we had so many in the house."

"The Sumner Branch Library (the only thing which still survives in my old neighborhood)!" said Mae. "I read every book in that library."

Martha used to read by the light of the corner arc lamp which shone in her window, and Alice's husband said the first question Alice asked him was: Where is your library card? Yes, I thought, that was important. I remembered whole summers of reading, devouring books, engorging them—whole shelves of Dumas, Balzac, Trowbridge, Alcott, Dickens, Thackeray. One volume after another until my head bulged and my eyes ached.

So our world had been. What moved us out of it? When had we first understood there was something beyond these Victorian boundaries?

Mae knew it when she got her first job reading proof in a print shop. She was the only girl in the proofroom. The language made her blush.

Martha felt there had been no big shock when she graduated, but the depression meant she didn't go to college.

And Alice had married right in the midst of the depression.

"I suppose I went to sleep in some ways," said Linnea. "I didn't have any rude awakening."

So for the past—what of the future? What ideas did the circle have—and did they possess any of that stock of optimism which still motivated me?

Reuben was pessimistic. He felt we were using up our minerals and fuel. They were bound to run out. We still have a growing population. It was not at zero growth yet. And religion tells people to go on breeding children no matter whether they can support them or not. He saw no escape. We were going to run out of land, of everything. Millions of cars on the roads and no gas to run them. No way this could end without a debacle, a calamity.

Mae agreed with Reuben. We are too wasteful. We don't seem to care. If the wrong person presses the button the whole world goes up. She felt more and more sure as she read Revelations. The answer may be there. And we were becoming a second-class nation. The world had no respect for us. Yet she didn't feel pessimistic. It was just that the wrong people had gotten us into trouble.

Alice was disillusioned about our lawmakers. We had to live with what we have. That's what we had been doing all our lives, and the country must do that, too. We poured money into the third world and now they blamed us for the famines.

Mel took issue. Watergate was a dramatic illustration of the way people could change things and put a stop to stealing and bad government. People were tough-minded. They wanted truth and intelligence and honesty—the old virtues that make for stability and the kind of people they can trust. We went on living on our annuities and social security and said to the kids: We made a mess of it—you got to clean it up. Well, we had better spend the rest of our lives removing the mess. We made it.

How many years of peace had we had in our fifty years? Hardly any. That meant we have been pouring our resources down a rat hole. We've given our children the dirty end of the stick. It was up to us, not them, to put things straight.

Reuben criticized Alice. She had said people were not grateful for our aid. Well, look who we had helped: Batista, Greece before the Colonels were thrown out, Spain, Portugal— the dictators and the generals. Well, then, how could we be surprised if these people look on us as enemies?

"The Marshall plan was pretty good," Mel said, "but since Korea we have built a ring of American bases around the world. Our help is tied to arms."

Alice, Reuben asked, do you believe the CIA committed crimes?

Alice nodded her head. Yes.

"I believe they committed crimes on the assumption that

Margaret (Muggsy) Keeney, 1975 editor of The Polaris, *the school weekly at North Side High. Her heroine is Bernadette Devlin. (Courtesy,* IAN PATRICK)

all these things could be hidden from us," Reuben said. "It is an irresponsible group. It committed all kinds of crimes including murder."

We had wandered away from talk of the future. I brought the conversation back.

There is no indication, Reuben said, that fifty years from now we will have solved our problems. Not by solar power or anything like that.

And Linnea pointed to Kontiki—the ocean is becoming permeated with trash and oil.

The stupidity is obvious, Mel said. Now it's out in public.

Alice's husband thought there had to be an improvement in communications, an enlargement of our mental capabilities. The technological changes had been tremendous. It was a new and challenging world. We were going to be coming up, not going down.

"It's a smaller world now," said Mel. "The smaller the world the more important to have big people. Harold Stassen had one great idea—the surrender of national sovereignty. Let our kids be people of the world, not of a country."

We were quiet a moment then Alice burst out: "Oh, what a wonderful group this is!"

Alice's words stay in my mind after they leave. There *is* something tangible about the Minnesota spirit. It cannot be sheer coincidence that after fifty years we wind up around this old oak table, each of us with deep concern about our country, about mankind, about the world, about our future. I thought of the many nights of my boyhood, sitting around this same table, talking and arguing as we have this night. I have not talked with these friends for fifty years but there is no real change. We are what we were. Rather we are *more* what we were. I remember how we wrangled in *The Polaris* office on those long afternoons, arguing as we have tonight. We believed then that the world was divided into good and evil and that we were on the side of good, that man was perfectible and that we, young editors in high school, would help to perfect him. Not much change.

But we are the departing generation. What of those who follow on—can this spirit survive?

It is two nights later. I am sitting on the screen porch of my sister's house. There's a smell of roses from the garden. I am sitting with Muggsy and Bunny. Muggsy is Margaret Keeney. She is eighteen years old and she has just graduated from North High as the editor of *The Polaris*. Her father is a switchman on the Burlington railroad. She is a small girl and looks and acts like her heroine, Bernadette Devlin.

"I'm very rowdy," she says. She waves her hands as she

talks and sparks fly from her eyes. Bunny is Bernadine Orrben. She is seventeeen and has another year at North High. She, too, is an editor of *Polaris*. Her father is dead and her stepfather has retired. Her manner is quieter than Muggsy's. Both girls are Catholics, both transferred to North High from Ascension. North High is now fifty-eight percent white and forty-two percent minority, mostly blacks and Chicanos and Indians. The Minneapolis papers often carry stories about North High being a "problem school." Muggsy and Bunny disagree violently.

Bunny: I went to a Catholic high school, but I decided I wanted to get out of an all-white school. People said you go to North and you'll get beaten up. At first I was kind of afraid, but once you meet some of the kids you don't think of them as black or white, just as persons.

Muggsy: Race doesn't have much effect on how you learn. It does have a bad affect on the community's relationship with the school. Wonderful things are going on at North High. A lot of the blacks are pretty insecure but everybody in our group is doing the same thing. Nobody notices whether you are a little white girl or a little black girl. It doesn't make any difference. But it is true that if you are a little white girl, you may be afraid of going out with a black boy.

Bunny: Black females take offense if a white girl goes with a black boy. The individual needs the support of the group and the group doesn't like it. It's not the individual. I really think that will change. Not only the blacks but the whites and Chicanos.

Muggsy: I think our kids seek a mixture of color not to mention personalities. Of course, both of us are white Catholic females. Chicanos have a much harder time getting recognition. The Indians have a special spirit and it is so hard for them. They have their traditional problem—the old Indian drunk on the street. It's the label of the Indians and it is so hard to keep your image. But I can understand why they are so proud of their heritage. I'm so proud of my Irish background. I met the grandfather of one of the Chicano students. He is eighty-two years old and he rode with Pancho Villa. Whew! That's something to be proud of!

Bunny: Some classes are cut off from the rest of the students. For instance, Black African classes. I have a friend who is part Indian, part black and part French. She has more identity crises than anyone. She got into the African studies class. They were nice to her but later on they called her a honky.

Muggsy: We have so much fun with our teachers. You can

go to the men teachers and talk about personal things and call them by their first names. You can talk to them about things you can't talk to your parents about.

Bunny: The teachers are very young. They really have creative ideas. They are very relaxed.

Muggsy: Kids like to horse around. The older teachers can't take it.

Bunny: Lots of our teachers had hard luck growing up, our stories are familiar to them. They grew up in hard conditions in Minneapolis. Now they live in the suburbs. It's kinda nice.

Muggsy: They had the same problems we had growing up. Lots of people like to come back and work at North.

Bunny: Our journalism teacher says he would come to North even if he was kicked out of his job.

I ask about drugs.

Bunny: That's pretty much a past thing.

Muggsy: Lots of kids smoke marijuana. But this year you didn't smell dope in the stairwells. It's not such a big thing now. The principal told us—if you are under sixteen I'll call in your parents; if you are over sixteen I'll call in the police and you'll be kicked out of school.

It was a fad and now it is a small thing. Nobody can afford drugs, not real drugs. Hash was everywhere in my sophomore year. It's all gone. What I'm disappointed in is that kids are still smoking cigarettes a lot. I smoke a lot. One day we are all going to feel the effects.

Bunny: So much depends on the teachers. They see a problem and help out.

Muggsy: You learn a lot about life at North. I would have died if I had to go to another school.

I ask what they would like to do in life.

Muggsy: I like to write. It makes things come alive. I have three sisters and one brother. Linda has three children, Terry one and Tony one. After baby sitting for my sisters I don't want any children.

Why did her sisters marry?

Muggsy: They had this idea of what they wanted to do. They were happy when they met their husbands and a career wasn't so important. I wouldn't mind getting married if I met a man I loved, but kids are another thing.

What about women's lib?

Muggsy: A lot of girls, pretty girls, are just interested in smiling and being pretty and that's it. The women at North High are not so involved.

Bunny: A lot of guys at North are not liberated. They just go out with girls who are not liberated.

Muggsy: They are just looking for old world women. My brother has been looking for an old world woman but he has had to settle for a pretty liberated woman.

Bunny: The boys are figuring out how to get a job. That's on their minds. The women can always marry a rich man.

Muggsy: To me the important thing is being able to talk to somebody or touch somebody. There is something good about being able to touch each other. Music is playing and you have been working for eight hours on a play rehearsal and suddenly you start dancing and you throw your arms around somebody. First you feel that it is improper but the important thing is to touch and talk. We are happy kids. There's nothing wrong for a boy to say I love you or to cry and talk about how sad something is.

Bunny: There are lots of male chauvinists and female chauvinists, too. Female athletes have a real tendency that way.

Muggsy: About the world—I get frustrated but it's been around a long time. I think we are getting too smart. There's too much technology.

Bunny: Things are scary. A guy is getting ready to go to college. He has to go out and make a living and maybe tomorrow the city won't be there because somebody pushes a button. It scares me to think that maybe somebody will push a button and I won't be here and nobody will be here.

Muggsy: I haven't worried about those things too much. But the fact that the quality of life of my children or, rather, my sisters' children can be affected because of some foolish thing that some man did—I worry about that.

Bunny: It all depends on one man.

Muggsy: Somehow I would rather have the Chinese come over and have somebody conquer us and take us over rather than have my brother or someone I love be killed. I don't know anything about China or Russia, but I have faith in human people. Money we can be without. The house can burn down. People can die. But love cannot die.

Bunny: Catholics have changed a lot, too.

Muggsy: I want to stay a Catholic, it's a big part of my life. But the people that run my religion don't do it the way I want. I just don't see it the way my parents do. There is a priest at St. Boniface's. I like his approach. He will tell you your religion can be used as a crutch but a crutch can be thrown away. And so can many things. The older generations didn't raise any questions.

Bunny: One of my sisters went to Good Shepherd. They are involved with wayward girls. She is about thirty and she is beginning to get it together. My older sister is thirty-two and she is still one half in the dark.

Muggsy: I wanted to be a nun when I was eight years old. How I wanted to be a nun! But I grew out of it.

I ask the girls about politics.

Muggsy: Kids want to be independent. I'd hate to say I'd vote for a Democrat just because my parents were Democrats. I'd like to figure out things for myself. I know I'm a lot more raucous than my mother. If I want to do something I'm going to do it even if she doesn't want me to. You grow up and you hear the Democrats are going to run the country into so much debt, but you know the Republicans do all they can for big business.

Bunny: A couple of years ago Mondale was going to all the schools, and he would have his picture taken with the kids and you knew what he was up to. That was too much. Maybe he is good but . . .

Muggsy: I was for Humphrey but I guess it is too much for him and he is getting old. I was really high on [Governor Wendell] Anderson, but in recent times he's been sort of mixed up. He hasn't been so good on the environment.

I ask about Teddy Kennedy.

Muggsy: I feel bad that Kennedy had to rip off a lot of people. I want to put my faith in Ted Kennedy. I suppose it shouldn't matter but I can't put my faith in someone who would cover up. I believed in Bobby. But I'd have to say that I would vote for Teddy with a little hesitation.

Bunny: To read about Jackie in the paper—I suppose she is a great woman but to read all those things in the paper is too much.

What about pregnancy in the school?

Muggsy: It's not a problem but it happens a lot. Kids deal with it. A lot of girls think of it not as having a man's kid. Maybe they don't have the kid on purpose, but most of them have the child. They don't give it up. It used to be that if you had a kid, they would refuse to let you in the course. But it is so nice now. No problem.

Bunny: Now they bring the little kids to school and the

little brothers and sisters if there's no one at home to look after them. A few of the boys and girls get married in school. One of my friends had a kid and then in the summer she got pregnant again so they got married.

Muggsy: Of course the girls go on to school except for the last weeks of pregnancy.

Bunny: The girls bring their kids to school. Maybe some of the teachers don't like it, but it's lots of fun playing with them.

Muggsy: And the boys, you know, some of them don't like to take care of diapers and stuff like that. Others are great. Most of the boys are attached to their children. They care a lot.

Muggsy and Bunny hope that they can go on to college. Muggsy is crazy about the theater. In high school she divided her time between theater classes and *The Polaris*. But she's never been able to afford to see a play at the Guthrie theater. She hopes she may be able to earn enough money to go to St. Cloud State College "but I'm not psyched up on it." She likes the idea of a smaller campus and she has some friends there, but it's hard being fifth in a family of five. Her mother works in a drugstore five days a week to help support the children. Bunny will go to college, too, if the money is there. She had a job when she was sixteen but she gave it up. Now she would fight anybody to get it back. Money is scarce in the families of Muggsy and Bunny.

After the girls have said good night I run over my notes. Muggsy and Bunny could be Linnea and Martha talking in 1925: the same spirit, the same eyes wide open to the world and the minds, fresh as a November wind. You don't have to know Bernadette Devlin is Muggsy's heroine to know that her motto is: dare to struggle, dare to die.

These girls have a purity of thought, an honesty of outlook on the world, a fresh clear-eyed conscience which shames me. I did not have their kind of courage when I was their age. I did not think so straight. My mind was full of woolly posturing, show-offism. I thought that the reason I could not really remember the long arguments I used to have with my *Polaris* companions was that we were not talking about real-life questions. I had been a poet in high school but I did not dare look up any of my verses in *The Polaris* weekly. I knew that their chief characteristic was banality.

Listening to these Minnesota girls I became certain of one thing. There was a Minnesota spirit and it was not only alive today—it had a maturity and a content far richer than it possessed fifty years ago.

The cry of those being eaten by America,
Others pale and soft being stored for later eating.

         —Robert Bly, 1970

The car is racing straight west on Minnesota 7, die straight from Minneapolis across the June landscape, brown and black fields of plowed land and the green of winter wheat, farm after farm, a cluster of willows, maples and cottonwoods around the houses, everywhere lilacs up to the second-story windows, big steel silos, deep blue enamel silos, slim corn cribs rusty with last year's cobs, the barns, the barricades of red-and-yellow machinery.

I am heading west to talk to Robert Bly, the poet, Minnesota's brooding genius. His words tear at our souls, although the editor of a weekly paper in South Dakota, fifteen miles from Bly's farm at Madison, has never heard of him.

This is a day for thunder showers and wind and sunshine, for meadowlarks and bobolinks and red-winged blackbirds. There are fat ducks in the buffalo wallows, quail at the roadside and mourning doves.

I am driving straight west to talk to Bly. I have met Bly before and I need his deep Norwegian pessimism, his Jungian analysis to temper the heady Minnesota spirit reverberating in my mind. He was born on the farm where he still lives at the very edge of the state up against the South Dakota border. He knows the land, he knows the people. He has lived among farmers and small-town folk his whole life. He is no romantic.

We cross the Minnesota river, wide and slow and darkly beautiful. I notice few cattle on the land, here and there Black Angus being fed, and small clusters of horses. Now we enter Lac Qui Parle Country—I have never seen it before—almost to Madison, turn off on a gravel road and come up to Robert Bly's house under the cottonwood trees.

It seems to be filled with kids—kids everywhere, two on the steps, red-haired and blonde, boys and girls, six in all, four of the Blys' and two are Ruth's who lives with them. The three adults divide their days of work. Today is Bly's and Ruth's. Carol Bly has a day of rest.

Bly is a big man, a strong man. He wears a tan shirt, dark trousers, a flowered tie. His wife has just come home from teaching Sunday school to the tiny Episcopal church. Bly has been with her.

He is deep into Jung. He talks about the male and female principles. The male principle has been badly dented by the

Vietnam war. Youngsters withdraw from the conflict, deny their masculinity and now sometimes they are castrated spiritually by strong females.

I don't understand all his philosophy but the words pour out. The young are infantile. They are concerned with their own bodies. Don't hurt me—they say—I'm all I've got. Kent State and Jackson State suddenly taught them what they had not realized—that they could lose their body and that it was all they had. They began to pull back and they are still pulling back. Nothing is more important to them than "I." They do not want to put "I" on the line. Not for anything.

The father concept, Bly says, was disgraced by Vietnam and women are taking over the male consciousness. Now we have a society without the father. It is the rise of the matriarchy.

What, I ask, do the farmers of Madison think about such reasoning. Bly has never given a poetry reading in this town where his father farmed a lifetime but last winter he gave a lecture course. Admission was four dollars and forty people attended. The subject: The Discoveries of Freud and Jung and How They Relate to Life in Madison, Minnesota. I think Bly was surprised to find the townspeople so open to his philosophy. They thought Freud exciting and Jung a great man, both helpful in their daily life, their problems of marriage, getting along with bosses and trying to get some new thinking into the high school.

But who are the people in Lac Qui Parle County? It is the least prosperous of the Minnesota farming communities. The farmers are getting older. (Their average age in North Dakota is fifty-three.) Young people are being driven out by the banks. They can't afford the land and the machinery. A University of Minnesota study estimated that to go into commercial farming in Minnesota last year required capital of $250,000, not counting start-up expenses.

"Young people can't afford that," Bly says. "Actually the banks dictate everything. They say whether you can have credit to buy a new machine and what it will be. They say what you will plant. Otherwise no loan for machinery, fertilizer and seed."

You have to farm 900 acres to be prosperous, 600 to make a living. A quarter section, 320 acres, puts you at subsistence level. Every year the number of acres needed to break even increases. It has been increasing since I was a boy. Then 160 acres was a very rich farm.

So the farmers today stay with corn and soy beans and

Robert Bly, the poet. Minnesota's brooding genius whose words tear at our souls—a man who faces evil squarely, calling it name for name.

short-feed cattle. There's not much grain anymore and the older farmers have problems. They haven't the energy to bale the straw after the harvest. Youngsters start to drink in sixth grade. Everyone drinks in the vacant houses in the countryside, vacated by the cannibalizing of farms. Party houses, they call them. The kids drink in them, bust them up, burn them down. Yesterday the paper reported a young man and woman died in a vacant farmhouse that burned down after a weekend of drinking. Only one in three or four farmhouses are used any more. They aren't needed with the big farms and all that machinery. The barns are kept for storage.

You've got to have $60,000 of your own to invest to get into farming and you have to give up your independence to the banks. Agriculture has been going downhill for thirty or forty years, straight downhill. The fathers enjoyed working the land but schoolteachers taught the sons that physical labor was bad, that they should go on to "higher things." That means that three quarters of the students stayed dissatisfied for the rest of their lives, despising physical labor. Minnesota has lost 85,000 farms since 1930 and yet the land devoted to agriculture has grown.

Everything depends on fertilizers now—anhydrous fertilizers. You start using them and lands get hooked just as people are hooked on drugs.

But what, I ask, about the old populist spirit that filled Minnesota when I was young, the spirit of hatred for the banks, for Wall Street, for the East, for Bigness, for Big Corporations and Big Business? The spirit that produced the Nonpartisan League and the Farmer-Labor Party?

Bly shakes his head. The people go with the system. They are submissive. Disciplined. They want to do what the neighbors do. They want to emulate the rich and the successful. Things have changed since the early Norwegians came over. The ones who came were not the Number-one sons. The Number-one sons got the family land. The Number-two sons came to Minnesota. They were filled with anger at the old order and they transferred some of the rage to the USA. Then the second wave of immigration brought the intelligentsia, the principled opponents of the Scandinavian establishment, followers of Ibsen. They were for socialism and social change. This was the mixture that was infused into Minnesota along with the Yankees and the Swedes and the Danes and the Germans. But that has thinned out with the years.

Still, the people in Madison are open to Bly's philosophy and there is no more savage critic of the American system of killing (not just Vietnam) and the American system of hypocrisy ("The ministers lie, the professors lie, the television lies, the priests lie").

Bly believes we have, as a nation, swallowed the big lump of Vietnam and that it has lodged in our belly. It will fester there and come back to haunt us as the Indians (whom we slaughtered) have come back to haunt us.

There is in Bly that deep strain of Norwegian pessimism, that black Scandinavian anger that was brought to Minnesota by the earlier generation along with a determination to face evil squarely, calling it name for name.

I drive back the three hours to Minneapolis through thunderstorms that fill the pearl-gray sky with black-uddered clouds and split the horizon with lightning, rain blinding the windshield. On this western prairie, life is painted in harsher contrasts than around the comfortable coffee tables of the cities. But, I am convinced, this is the kind of honesty we must have if the swollen lumps of Vietnam and the other horrors are to pass finally through our system. They will not pass without pain and the mark will stay with us for years. But is that not just? After the agony we have inflicted on others must we not pay the reckoning? Why should we suppose that there is some kind of exceptionalism that permits us to kill and destroy and live unscathed in body and mind?

The American democracy is long-suffering and slow in rousing itself, it is often perplexed by problems and seems to grope blindly for their solution.
—*James Bryce*, THE AMERICAN COMMONWEALTH, *1888*

The first time I saw Wendell Anderson he had just put a green-and-orange voyageur's cap on Hubert Humphrey's head and tied a green-and-orange voyageur's sash around Humphrey's solid waist. Then he did the same to me. He was entertaining the Governors' Conference and this was horseplay at a cookout on a Mississippi sandbar below old Fort Snelling.

Anderson has reddish hair, a freckled face, clear blue eyes, a quizzical grin, and looks like a hockey player, which he was until he became Minnesota's governor.

I wanted to talk to him because he is young and thoughtful and many people think he embodies the "Minnesota spirit," if indeed, there is such a thing. He had just come back by helicopter from inspecting some flooded farmlands near Waseca in southern Minnesota and was filled with the problems of the farmers. "I'm a city boy myself," he says, but he is the product of Swedish grandparents who came to farm in Minnesota in the 1890s; one set of grandparents from northern Sweden, the other from the lake country sixty miles north of Göteburg.

Anderson talks with an air of authority, his blue eyes piercing you as the words come out rapidly and crisply.

Bly is right. There is a problem about farming in Minnesota and in the other parts of the heartland. Agribusiness has moved in. But Anderson has gotten legislation approved to keep the problem in hand. The growth of existing corporate farms has been limited and in new enterprises the majority must be Minnesotans. It's not perfect but it's a start. He has been looking at the Saskatchewan system, where the state buys land and sells to qualified local farmers on decent credit. The problem is how to pick the people to buy state farmlands? There are sure to be a lot more buyers than land.

Why not a lottery, I suggest. He shakes his head. Yes, this might be the answer. In any event Minnesota is not California where much of the land—and most of the best land—is now in the hands of corporate giants.

As for young people—it is true that there is a back-to-the-farm movement. They want to go to the country and work with their hands. A good many young professional people in Minnesota work part time on their farms in the country. It's an attractive way of life.

Is there, I ask, anything to the idea that there is a Minnesota spirit, a Minnesota particularity?

There is. Anderson's eyes light up. It comes from the unusual mixture of the Scandinavian emigration of the '80s, '90s and 1900s and the early New England tradition. All these people came from lands of difficulty and hardship. Many of the New Englanders came from Maine and its rocky upland farms, the Scandinavians from the same kind of country. The mixture bore fruit in the agrarian populist movements—the Farmer-Labor Party in Minnesota, the Nonpartisan League in North Dakota, the La Follette progressives in Wisconsin. The merger of the Farmer-Labor Party with the Democrats revitalized the Democrats.

Minnesota has a tradition of youth in politics. It goes back to Floyd Olson, Harold Stassen, Hubert Humphrey, Eugene McCarthy. George McGovern comes out of the same tradition. The average age of members of the Minneapolis City Council is under thirty. There is a steady attraction of young people into politics and for this great credit must be given to Humphrey. Humphrey has to be the most humane and human man in American politics, a whole generation of young Minnesota politicians is in his debt. (Anderson, I know, is a Humphrey protégé.)

There is an interesting custom among the big corporations in Minnesota. Almost all except for those which own the iron ore in the north are Minnesota-owned and they are based in Minnesota, in Minneapolis and St. Paul. They permit their young engineers and technical specialists to go into politics.

The Speaker of the House has this background. So do several brilliant young legislative leaders. Of course, the corporations fight higher taxes. Of course, they are conservative. But their influence is not antagonistic to good government. They are not absentee landlords and they have a sense of responsibility. Even if they fight higher taxes they do pay them and they realize that this benefits the community and creates a desirable atmosphere. The streets in Minneapolis and St. Paul are clean.

And, he could have added, downtown Minneapolis is no urban slum like many city cores—it is a light and imaginative construct of lifting skyscrapers (a beautiful Philip Johnson tower), skyways that link the downtown banks, department stores and hotels and pedestrian shopping malls. The university, the symphony orchestra, the Guthrie Theater, the Walker and Minneapolis art galleries, give it cultural vitality.

Politics is clean. There has been no major conviction of a political figure for graft as far back as anyone can remember. It is clean competitively, too. The modern corporations are not like the old railroad and timber barons who bought legislatures, governors and tax officials. There is no political dynasty in the state. The politicians are young men. All are poor. They made their own way. They have to win the acceptance of their peers. Before he was finally nominated, Anderson had been examined and questioned three or four times by each of the 1,200 delegates at the state convention.

Of course this is not all perfect. He doesn't like monopolies of communications—one company owning many papers, radio and TV stations. There should be diversity of news. He'd like to see divestment of some of the big monopolies.

Minnesota spends lots of money on education. Anyone can be popular shouting against taxes. But you can't have good government and service to and for people without taxes. Service to the people. That is the purpose of government. We must work to free the land, the cities, the rivers and the air of pollution. We must preserve our basic farming communities. Land is the foundation of our whole life. We must not forget that.

Anderson thinks back to the days when he was growing up. In those times, he says, Sunday was a free day, a family day. We worked hard all week long. But on Sunday no one worked. Now with all the leisure in our lives Sunday is becoming blurred. People work all the time or play all the time. Some people do still set Sunday or Saturday aside for religious observance. That is fine. But there should be one time for rest and

Once European travelers thought Lake Pepin, on the upper Mississippi, a sight unequaled. Now, off the highways, it is neglected, unknown. (Courtesy, MINNESOTA DEPARTMENT OF ECONOMIC DEVELOPMENT)

relaxation. We ought to figure out a way to do this on a national basis. It sounds like a nostalgic idea to me but appealing, perhaps, because of that.

He thinks the mood of the American people is serious. They want serious answers and they know the problems are serious. Watergate has made them think. The old politics isn't good enough. Politicians have to know what they're talking about. Minneapolis and St. Paul aren't laying off police, and the reason is simple. State help. The state is giving them $10,000,000 aid from state income-tax funds. The tax is high but we use it to keep the state healthy.

He doesn't use Bly's language about Vietnam, but what he says comes to the same thing—we have to face up to the fact that we have spent $150- to $250 billion on Vietnam. We have neglected every problem at home—the cities, the farms, youth, jobs. We must have jobs, not relief. Relief is the most inflationary thing in the world. Everyone able to work should be guaranteed a job—naturally the pay should be below the commercial rate in order to encourage people to get private jobs.

We move out of the big dark restaurant. I don't know whether it's a politicians' hangout or not, but everyone knows the Governor. They greet him and he waves a friendly hand. Some kids stop him on the street outside and ask for his autograph.

Yes, he says, going back to the basic question. There is a Minnesota spirit and we will keep it alive.

In Hiram's day the Fourth of July was *the* holiday. He never mentioned Christmas, just recording what he happened to be doing on December 25, getting a stack of hay for his horse, folding almanacs in his brother's printing establishment or butchering his hogs. He recorded New Year's Day every year and once noted twenty-six cents in expenses for its celebration—probably for rum. But the Fourth of July was another thing. This was the "Anniversary of Independence" and he not infrequently mentioned going to Chepachet for a celebration. In 1815, July 4, 1776, was only thirty-nine years in the past.

I grew up to venerate the Fourth. I always woke up early on the holiday, sometimes before the sun was fully up. By six I had routed my father out of bed and the two of us would ascend to the attic, the sun slanting through the elms outside and no small boys yet awakened to set off Minnesota limits, the three-inch firecrackers which were the largest legally sold. We would grub around in a dark cubbyhole under a gable, cobwebbed and smelling of mothballs and my grandfather's old medical cabinet, draw out the big flag on its heavy oak pole and put it out the small window in the front of the attic, fitting it firmly into the iron stanchion imbedded in the floor. Then I would run down the back staircase into the alley and around the house to see how it looked. It looked splendid! It always did.

Today that kind of thing is thought to be very old fashioned. The flag can be seen almost anywhere you look—in a Jasper Johns painting or on the backside of a pretty girl, but there's not much left of Fourth of July—the great picnics and the hours of political oratory which accompanied the potato salad, the soda pop and the bellyaches of the youngsters.

It is almost gone. But not quite. On July 4, 1975, I drove to Sharon, Connecticut, where, I had read, there was going to be a village Fourth of July celebration. It was a sunny clear day like the Fourth of Julys of my youth. Sharon is an old town of white houses in the foothills of the Berkshires and the celebration was being held on the village green, an oblong about one-hundred feet wide and two blocks long, an expanse of well-tended grass in the center of town. On one side are set-back houses, on the other the town hall, the church and some small shops. There is a certain mythology about the Sharon Green. For three years this was the scene of the Sharon Peace Vigil. From November 29, 1969, to January 27, 1973, every Saturday morning at 11 A.M. a band of local villagers and occasional recruits from outside stood silently at the green or walked in a solemn procession around its perimeter, protesting the Vietnam war. Sometimes as few as eight stalwarts turned out on wintry Saturdays, sometimes the numbers swelled to one-hundred and fifty. There were occasional tense moments. Sharon is sometimes called the baronial seat of the Buckley clan, which resides in four great and beautiful mansions just down from the green. The Buckleys and not a few Sharon residents felt as strongly for the war as did the Vigil members against it. No actual violence occurred but in the early days of the Vigil, pro-war partisans sometimes drove past the green, lights on, honking horns and giving vent to occasional epithets.

Nothing quite like the Sharon Vigil occurred anywhere else in the United States. It ended only with the cease-fire and the American pull-out, and this was in my mind as I drove up to the green on Fourth of July morning just before noon.

I found possibly one-hundred people spread out across the lawn. There were many children and lots of people spread blankets to protect their clothes against grass stains. A man in a red shirt and broad-brimmed hat was standing beside a restored Ford Model-T, its brass work gleaming in the sunshine. Stands had been decorated in red-white-and-blue and sold cold soda and cold ears of corn, each for thirty cents. The four columns of great elms which once shaded the green have all vanished, victims of Dutch elm disease, but the surviving maples still provide shade. Across from the green stands a two-story town hall of red brick with white columns and a three-story tower. Next door is a neat old red-brick building, which used to house the Sharon post office.

At noon the town siren sounded and two Scouts, a boy and a girl, their chests laden with merit badges, raised the flag as everyone sang a verse of America. The chairman announced that Sharon was the one-hundred and sixty-ninth of the one-hundred and sixty-nine towns in Connecticut to accept the official flag honoring the nation's two-hundredth anniversary. "We're pretty independent around here," he observes. "That's why we call it Independence Day." There is an appreciative chuckle from the crowd.

William Landers, who directs the Sharon Playhouse, a summer theater, steps forward. He is wearing a white shirt, a red tie and blue serge trousers. His beard is grey and his head baldish. He reads the Declaration of Independence—not the official version but Jefferson's original draft. The crowd stands at rapt attention as Landers, with his actor's voice, reads out the old words, somehow investing them with the freshness of yesterday. The interest rises as he reads the Jeffersonian phrases stricken by Congress:

"We must endeavor to forget our former love for them [the British] and hold them as we hold the rest of mankind enemies in war, in peace friends. We might have been a free and a great people together; but a communication of grandeur and of freedom, it seems, is below their dignity. Be it so, since they will have it. The road to happiness and to glory is open to us, too. We will tread it apart from them and acquiese in the necessity which denounces our eternal separation."

There is a hush when the speaker concludes. Even the children are silent. Then folk singers take up the haunting words of "Johnny Has Gone for a Soldier" and they sound over the green, where in 1776 not a few Sharon Johnnys gathered in ragged platoons and, too, went for a soldier.

I walked back to my car. The rest of the day would be devoted to the classics of Fourth of July—children's games, square dancing, a raffle, an auction of cakes. It was the seventy-sixth Fourth of July picnic to be held on the village green, a young ceremony for this old community, which itself celebrated its two-hundredth birthday in 1939. Elsewhere the Fourth of July might have turned into a festival of sunburn, traffic jams and beach excursions, but the spark of old country patriotism has not flickered out. Hiram would have felt at home on the Sharon Green, although he might have been a bit puzzled at the funny "colonial" hats which were being sold as souvenirs. Patriotism—stated patriotism—is not in style today, but what could symbolize America better than the Sharon

Green with its homely demonstrations of principled differences, against the war, for the war. What better than this simple rededication to those plain truths so eloquently fashioned by Jefferson? It was *my* kind of Fourth of July.

> To Mr. H. Salisbury, future journalist & editor
> Good luck,
> Always
> *Farrell Dobbs*
>
> (*Inscription in 1925* POLARIS *ANNUAL*)

I see a spry, spare man watering a small lawn in front of a bungalow in a dead-end street not far from the Berkeley turn-off across the bay from San Francisco. I'm not sure about the address and I go past and then come back. The sun is shining. It is very hot. The man is wearing a red-and-purple plaid sports shirt, blue trousers and sandals. He is Farrell Dobbs and he ran for the Presidency of the United States four times on the ticket of the Socialist Workers Party.

When I talked with Mae Rockne Cruys about the fiftieth reunion of North Side High, I asked her if we didn't have any famous people in our class, any famous criminals or great heroes. Mae thought of one man who had been sent to jail for running over his wife with his car. That was the only big court case she could think of. But as for famous people, well, we'd had a Presidential candidate, Farrell Dobbs.

The name came back to me, but I had not remembered he was my classmate. Both he and I were surprised to find we had written in each other's high-school annual.

Farrell Dobbs retired a year ago with his wife, Marvel Erickson, to California after a life-time of struggle against the system. He was an authentic revolutionary. He'd known Trotsky and in 1940 had inspected Trotsky's Mexican stronghold and twice had tried to improve its security, but nothing he had done served to protect Trotsky from Stalin's assassin.

How, I asked, as we sat in the living room of the little house, the bookcase filled with paperback Trotskys, Isaac Deutscher and a few B. Traven novels, Farrell sitting in a maple rocking chair, Marvel on a green couch and the faint sound of semiclassical music in the background, had it all come about? How had he become a revolutionary and what had life taught him?

Fifty years, Farrell said, was a long time. Everyone comes to get older and no one has that fresh-eyed naiveté and feeling that the world is his oyster that we all had when we got out of North Side High.

His father had been an independent teamster and trucker. He probably scabbed during the 1916 teamsters' strike in Minneapolis. They lived in a rural slum called Bowling Green on the edge of Minneapolis, just north of Keegan's Lake, where my mother had grown up. He went to Lincoln School and like all of us borrowed books at Sumner Library.

There wasn't money for Farrell to go to college when he graduated in 1925 and he and Marvel got married. Her stepfather was a Debs socialist and he'd kicked a Liberty Loan salesman out of the house during World War I. Marvel was so frightened for her mother that she became a violent supporter of the war and "very conservative." Farrell had no politics at all. He got a job with Western Electric, and was moving ahead. He'd been transferred to Omaha. One day the company fired an old man who was a senior employee. The idea was to save his high salary and avoid paying him a pension when he retired.

"I told Marvel I didn't want any part of that," Farrell said. He quit his job. They had saved about five-hundred dollars and he decided to go to law school at the university so he could become a judge. Then, he thought, somehow he'd be able to help people and end such unjustice as he had just witnessed. A naive idea, perhaps, but they put their money into a little dry-cleaning business and promptly lost it. Marvel was two months pregnant. Farrell got a job selling insurance, but he lost that, too. He refused to sell his poor customers the expensive insurance the company wanted to push. Finally, his father got him a job at sixteen dollars a week, shoveling coal in the Pittsburgh coal yards. One day a man named Grant Dunne came in to load his truck and began to talk about unions. Farrell knew nothing about unions, in fact, thought they were something like lodges, the Elks or the Moose. But what Dunne told him seemed to make sense. The working men would be able to speak with one voice. Farrell joined up and that winter of 1934—on a day in February when the temperature was thirty below zero (and everyone wanted coal)—the workers struck and won their fight in three days. With spring it was a different story—the strike leaders, including Farrell, were laid off.

Grant Dunne was one of three brothers to become famous in the radical organizing activities of the teamsters union. The Dunnes had been socialists during World War I, then joined the

Communist Party with most of the Minnesota Socialists after the Russian Revolution. With the split in the Russian party they followed Trotsky. In a few weeks time Farrell became a Trotskyite, although he would have been hard put to explain a Trotskyite's political philosophy.

But he learned fast. In May, 1934, there was a violent strike in Minneapolis, led by the three Dunnes. Police used riot guns, two men were killed and more than fifty wounded. I had left Minneapolis by then but I remembered the strike. There was a full military confrontation with the National Guard. My father thought civil war was breaking out. No telling what the Reds would do next. The union leadership was arrested, but Grant Dunne and Farrell escaped and carried on from the underground—setting up command posts at filling stations and changing them a dozen times a day.

"It was a cram course in revolutionary warfare," Farrell recalls. "Not a dry classroom lecture."

Marvel is still hot tempered. She remembers trying to go up the stairs at teamster headquarters during the excitement. Eric Sevareid—she still calls him by his old Minneapolis name, Arne Severeid—and several reporters picked her up and pretended they were going to throw her over the staircase. She has never forgiven him. Neither of them ever forgave the radical governor, Floyd Olson, whom they believe tried to play both sides during the worst moments of the struggle.

We sat down to lunch—liver sausage, salami, cheese, rye bread, lettuce and tomato salad, chocolate ice cream and chocolate cookies and tea. Farrell doesn't use salt on doctor's orders; Marvel doesn't eat ice cream. I noticed *The Spoon River Anthology* on the bookcase. It is one of Farrell's favorites.

At North High, Farrell says, none of us were aware of the nuances of life. Equality of opportunity didn't quite exist because of economic differences, but we were alike in that we all thought we were going to find our place in life. We didn't have too many preconceived ideas. We felt that we were going to see what life was like when we got out of school. We'd make our decisions as we went along. Those that fared worst were the ones who permitted their parents to impose their fate on them. They wound up as Babbits. They were the least fortunate. They were stripped of all rights of self-determination.

But for those of us who went out on our own in the quest of the future it was marvelous. We had been looking forward to this all our lives. Now we were earning our own money and doing what we wanted to do.

The conversation turned back to the teamsters. After the big strikes, Farrell said, it was obvious that the movement would roll across the country and it did—the San Francisco General Strike, the Cleveland Autolite Strike and the big drive to organize the CIO. The working class was reacting and when you looked beyond Minneapolis, you saw the same thing going on out in the country. Not until 1936 and 1937 did Farrell have time to begin reading about socialism, Trotsky and the Third International. He was traveling around the country organizing the over-the-road truckers and had a chance to read at night and then in 1940 he went into full-time work for the Socialist Workers Party. These were the days when he went to Mexico and saw Trotsky. He tried to improve the training of the guards. He took them out on the desert and set up a target. While he was fixing the target someone started shooting and nearly blew his head off. He had put up two gun turrets to protect Trotsky's house after it was attacked by machinegun fire. He met the young man who killed Trotsky but neither he nor anyone else thought of him as a danger.

Then came World War II and everything changed. The Government brought suit against the whole top leadership of the Socialist Workers Party. The jury found them guilty on December 6, 1941. They were sitting around headquarters on Sunday afternoon, December 7, playing pinochle when the news of Pearl Harbor came in.

"I knew we were through then," Farrell says a bit sadly. "I knew we might be in jail for the rest of our lives."

It wasn't quite the rest of their lives, but it might as well have been so far as the movement was concerned.

They got sixteen months in the Sandstone, Minnesota, penitentiary. They appealed but finally went to jail on December 31, 1943, and were not released until the end of June, 1945. Farrell spent his time studying French and Spanish. By now, Farrell said, his "consciousness" had advanced and he understood that the only course was to break with the Republican and Democratic parties and found a party of labor. But the party had been smashed. It never came back.

"What do you do in a time like that?" Farrell said. "You try to conduct public and propaganda activities as best you can. You take what advantages you can. You study. You enrich yourself."

The FBI kept an eye on them. Marvel got telephone calls in the middle of the night. Matter of fact, Farrell said, the FBI probably still keeps an eye on them.

In forty-one years of political life he had learned some things.

"Many people are more wounded than they realize because they don't look outside themselves," he reflected. "They see everything in relationship to themselves. If you can do someone an act of kindness then you lift yourself a bit out of yourself."

Things began to change, Farrell thinks, in the 1960s, touched off by the Supreme Court's decision in 1954 in *Brown* v. *The Board of Education*. Then came the bus boycott, the mass movement against Jim Crow laws. He went down South and donated his station wagon to the civil rights movement. When the Cuban revolution came in 1960, he went to Cuba. The July 26th movement was heavily dependent on the Russians (sworn enemies of the Trotskyites). Still he got along well, possibly because he was a friend of revolution. And he began to find more interest on campuses. He got invited to speak. The Socialist Workers paper, *The Militant*, gained a bit of circulation. Students joined up. During the 1960s the party got new blood from the new generation of young rebels. It was time for a change in leadership. Some students from Carleton College in Minnesota had come up to Minneapolis and talked to Ray Dunne. Most came from working-class families. They joined the party and from these young cadres and others like them the new ranks of the party would be drawn.

What, I ask, are the prospects for Revolution in America?

The years have not blunted Farrell's optimism. He still sees success glimmering at the edge of the horizon. He thinks the prospects are better than at any time since the 1930s. In the 1930s there hadn't been any mass radicalization. Now we have had a long period of economic prosperity, but our prosperity is honeycombed by cyclical depressions. We are closer than ever to a shock like that of 1930. At the moment people have a sense of caution, but in the long run society is unsettled. The minorities are becoming radicalized—the blacks, the Puerto Ricans, the Chicanos. The American Indian movement has had a wide effect on young people as well as Indians. The women's liberation movement has become important. The movements even reach into the homes of the heads of great corporations, their wives and children are caught up. Out of these forces, he still believes, will arise the revolution of the future.

As for himself and Marvel, they've passed the baton to the young. Their three daughters live around Berkeley. This was Mother's Day and they trooped by with flowers for Mom. Farrell is writing the last of three autobiographical books about the movement. They like the atmosphere of Berkeley. It is quiet. They will live longer.

Marvel remembers something. She wrote a story about an Indian massacre when she was at North High. She had hoped to make *The Polaris*—but she didn't.

I wonder as I drive back across the bridge to San Francisco. Farrell has spent his life as a leader of a party dedicated to the cause of revolution in the United States, a party which draws its formal ideology from that fractional body of the Bolshevik Communist Party which sprang into being almost fifty years ago as the product of the bitter rivalry between Stalin and Trotsky. He thinks changes can come about only by Revolution. But what are the changes he wants—do they differ today so much from what the rest of those I've spoken with hope to gain through the existing political process? Not really. How much different are Farrell's ideals from those with whom I have been discussing the Minnesota spirit? Not much. I had asked Marvel and Farrell about the origin of the Minnesota spirit and Marvel's reply was not different from the others I had heard. She believes it sprang out of the mixture of emigration—the large social democratic strain among the immigrants from Scandinavia, Germany and Finland who had come to the state with its New England background. This is why so much of Minnesota politics had always been what is called left of center. Other movements had risen up—the native IWW, with its ideology of struggle and the tradition of syndicalism. In no other part of the country had a political movement based on an alliance of workers and farmers captured a position as high as that of governor.

What might have happened if Grant Dunne had not wandered into the Pittsburgh coal yard that winter day and began talking to the wiry young man loading the coal with his No. 10 shovel?

There was, it seemed to me, a common strand which joined these Minnesota people—Robert Bly, Mel Frank and my North High classmates, Governor Anderson and the Minnesota politicians who had come before, Olson, Stassen (who had headed my own campus political faction at the University), Humphrey (who had been mayor of my own city, Minneapolis) and the rest—and Muggsy and Bunny as well. It was a philosophy that I shared. However they might express it, they believed in the perfectability of man and they believed that this was a goal worth fighting for; worth, if necessary, dedicating your life to. Nothing in fifty years had moved them away from that conviction. I did not think anything in the next fifty years would change the Minnesota spirit. It was, I thought, as natural a product of the heartland as the corn of Iowa. I had grown up with it and I could see no sign that it had lost its vigor. It was the kind of social thinking which I thought Hiram and those who had gone before would have found compatible with the world as they knew it.

6

What place is this, to which the squalid street conducts us? A kind of square of leprous houses . . . ruined houses, open to the street, whence through wide gaps in the walls, other ruins loom upon the eye, as though the world of vice and misery had nothing else to show, hideous tenaments. . . .
—*Charles Dickens*, AMERICAN NOTES, *1842*

ALL VERY WELL, I say to myself. The heartland is one thing. The Minnesota Spirit another. But this is not the whole of America. America is there in the headlines: crime, dope, disaster. The country is coming apart. The cities have turned into jungles. New York is finished. People are fleeing by the tens of thousands to the safe enclaves of the suburbs (where they live behind wove-wire barricades, electronic alarm systems, flood-lighted gates and terror), while I am spending my time lighting candles at the altar of a fusion of Scandinavian radicalism and Puritan ethic, which flourishes in the cornfields.

So I embark on another journey. This is one I have made before—down into the streets of New York to see what life actually goes on there. I know what the well-bred lady from Cleveland thinks. I sat next to her at dinner and she told me of her great distress. Born and raised in New York, she loved the city, loved everything about it. "But I wouldn't think of going there now," she says belligerently. "There's nothing left of the New York I knew. It's too frightening."

Perhaps. I have lived in Manhattan for many years. I ride

the subway to Times Square every day. I walk past the pimps in
fawn jackets and broad hats, the whores with their platform
shoes, I pass the porn flicks and the massage parlors, the
hustlers and the bug-eyed customers from out of town. I know
that *The Times* floodlights Forty Third Street and hires a pla-
toon of guards to protect the printers coming to and from work
(even so one was killed). I watch the streets (I know which *side*
of the street to walk on at certain hours) and don't cross Central
Park at midnight or ride alone in the last subway car. I've suffered the garbage strikes, the subway strikes, the taxi strikes,
the newspaper strikes, the blackouts, the brownouts, the water
crises, been burglarized, sworn at the high prices and the in-
convenience.

But I love New York, and when a woman in Philadelphia
tells me that she adored living in Greenwich Village but now
she is fifty and not twenty and was frightened to death spending
a weekend in an apartment at Madison Avenue and Seventieth
Street I bristle.

Yet, if I am wrong, if New York and the other great cities
are past salvation, the country is in worse trouble than I believe.
Maybe dedication to truth, honesty, hard work and perfectability isn't enough to do the job.

I am sitting in a taxi one day and the driver starts talking.
He's a chipper little man and I see by the license that his name
is Benjamin Cohen. He's eighty years old, he says, and he came
in this morning because no one else showed up for work. He
likes to work. He's been driving for thirty years. Before that he
worked on the Third Avenue Elevated Railroad and before that
he worked for Jack Dempsey's manager. He fought a couple of
times, but he learned it was no place for a Jewish boy. He grew
up on the Lower East Side around Delancey Street and went to
school on Fourteenth Street. In those days kids had respect for
the teacher. His teacher read the Bible—so what. It didn't do
him any harm and he's still Jewish.

He likes to walk for exercise. He's walked from Grand
Concourse to the Battery. "I've been mugged four times," he
says "and shot once." He was up on the Grand Concourse yesterday and saw some elderly people waiting for the bus. Mug-
gers came up and took their pocketbooks. "There ain't no cops
around," he says. "Nobody interferes. I picked up one of the
ladies' purses. There was a subway token and twenty-seven
cents in it."

He said that he had told his rabbi: "Okay, I'm Jewish and

we're not supposed to have any prejudices. You are all for helping these people, but they are just animals. They don't work."

He pauses a moment, shouldering his cab around a tractor-trailer.

"You'll be surprised at what I'm going to say. I'm surprised, too," he says. "But I've thought a lot about this. I think we ought to have a class system in this country. It's the only way. If you don't work—then go live in a slum. If you do work—you get the benefit of it. If you don't work—why should you be helped? I know, I know. It's a hell of a thing for a Jew to say. But there it is."

Benjamin Cohen said retirement was just slow death. He worked and he liked it. Always had. He had voted for Nixon. First time he ever voted for a Republican, but the other guy wanted to give everybody $1,000—what kind of a guy was that? So he voted for Nixon. What a bargain!

"What's the country coming to?" he mused. "I have my own place. You ought to see it at night. I put the ironing board and pails and everything else against the door. Nobody can break in."

We were pulling to the curb. Cohen said he was sorry to give me such a big blast. He was just an old New York taxi driver and he liked to get it off his chest. He smiled quizzically. He wasn't sore about anything. That was just the way things were.

The playright Arthur Miller is an old friend of mine and a native New Yorker. He grew up in Harlem and later on his family moved to Brooklyn. He'd been up to City College to give a talk. It was his old neighborhood and he thought he would catch a cab or the subway back to the Chelsea Hotel, where he was staying. He was waiting on the corner below City College when two black women approached him. They were on the faculty and they offered to go with him to the subway. Arthur turned down the offer. He is tall and powerfully built. He was not going to be escorted through his old neighborhood by a couple of middle-aged black teachers. This bothered them. They didn't think he ought to wait on the corner alone. No cabs came. He began to feel uncomfortable. The people on the street, he thought, had started to eye him in a peculiar way. Finally a wildcat cab appeared, a very beat-up cab. It stopped and a good-looking black girl got out. She looked in surprise when he came up: "You want this cab?" Arthur said yes. The driver was equally surprised. If he went down to Twenty-third

Street, he couldn't get a fare back uptown. Finally, Arthur promised a tip to make up for the empty ride back.

The driver had a curious accent and was, it turned out, an Ethiopian. He'd gotten his degree from Columbia last year. He couldn't go home because he'd be clapped in prison. So here he was driving a gypsy cab. At the Chelsea, Arthur and the Ethiopian spent a couple of hours talking over the state of the world.

"You have to remember," Arthur said, "New York is now two worlds. The world above One Hundred Twenty-Fifth Street (Harlem) and the world below it."

But as for crime—he didn't think things had changed a lot. When he was growing up in Harlem, you expected things to be stolen. If you put something down it would be stolen. When he went to the blackboard to recite he took his junk along with him, his overshoes, his boots, his stuff from his desk, and put it down while he recited.

He remembered when they moved to Brooklyn. The kid beside him didn't take his stuff to the blackboard. Nobody stole it. Arthur could hardly believe his eyes. Brooklyn, too, was the first place he realized that the school seats weren't meant for two children to sit on. He had one to himself.

No, he said, so far as crime is concerned—there's nothing new about that in New York. When he was growing up, everything was stolen—everything.

Fifteen years ago I had taken the Lexington Avenue Subway down to Canal Street and walked back into the old immigrant East Side that Jacob Riis had known and Lillian Wald and the turn-of-the-century reformers who set out to make New York City a fit place for human habitation. That was long before Albert Schweitzer had proclaimed that "modern man is lost in the mass in a way which is without precedent in history." But the shame of the cities was there, rooted in these narrow tenement streets, where generation after generation of immigrants had taken first refuge and lived in the loathsome conditions described by Dickens.

While I knew that nothing could match the evil of London in Dickens's day, it was hard for me to believe what I saw in the New York of the late 1950s.

I had picked several areas to explore: Red Hook, Brooklyn, Bedford-Stuyvesant (now steadily improving under the Kennedys' imaginative attention) and the old East Side. The problem was dramatic. Teen-age "bopping" gangs had taken over the streets. Hundreds of adolescent gangs fought bloody and fatal battles in the shadow of slum clearance projects and slum parks. Jittery police envisaged the day when the gangs might launch a general offensive, moving in from the South Bronx, coming up from the East Side, pouring over from Brooklyn. It was a vision which bore no relation to the reality of the half-starved, illiterate, wine-fused gangs. But it was enough to terrify the city. People could hardly believe I spent a winter hanging out with the street gangs on cold slum corners.

There were social theorists who sought to impose on the bopping clubs an image of the world around them, to see in their violence a crooked version of the real world, still deep in cold war, not long out of Korea, not yet plunged into Vietnam.

That didn't make sense to me. The kids I knew simply huddled together for comfort. The gangs might be aggressive to others; to themselves they were defensive and protective, and if they too often killed and wounded each other, stole property or defaced buildings that was the way of life in this alienated sub-culture.

One thing I did not doubt. These slums were the bottom of the giant antheap. If New York was on the skids, if New Yorkers were turning into "animals," if our civilization was on the brink, the place to find out was at the bottom where another world existed without romantic illusion.

Once again I went to Grand Central, paid fifty cents for a token (it had been twenty cents the last time I took this ride) and in ten minutes was walking up from the big Canal Street Station. This was old New York, the delight of the ethnic archaeologist. Here you could peel back the layers of immigration, the Irish imposed on the German layer, the Italians on top of that. In the nearby East River thousands of homeless orphans once burrowed in the hay barges by night, issuing in daytime to sell papers for Pulitzer or Hearst or snatch the purses of unwary ladies and gentlemen.

Now I walk east along Canal. Instantly I spy changes. The Chinese have flowed north over Canal Street and invaded the Italian streets. The Puerto Ricans just pouring into the region when I last came here now hold dominance in many streets. The shops on the north side of Canal displayed signs in two languages—Spanish and Chinese. I pause at the corner of Mulberry, heart of Little Italy. Four young Italians are carrying a big red-and-gray funeral wreath along the sidewalk, and I see two young Chinese walking north. The Chinese are pushing deep into Italian territory.

I am headed for Forsyth Street, which begins at the concrete base of Williamsburg Bridge and runs north. At the start of the street I walk around a man passed out on the sidewalk, his head resting in a pagoda of cardboard boxes and a khaki raincoat covering him.

I walk up Forsyth Street and pass a Chinese store next to a unisex hair-cutting establishment. A squad car is standing in front of PS 91 and two cops are talking at the door while a little Chinese girl stands on the sidewalk, staring into space. I pass a red-lettered Chinese storefront, the Jungle Social Club and Ponce Social Club.

On the west side of Forsyth lies Sara Roosevelt Park. For years it was an open excavation for a subway extension, children playing on the girders as though it were a jungle gym. It has been put back to rights now, after the New York fashion of slum parks, that is, acres of concrete and concrete benches. Not much else. For two or three years after the subway was finished, the city used the park to store salt for the streets in winter. I wonder if any of Sara Roosevelt's descendants have seen what has been done in her name.

Now I pass a burned-out tenement and then another. They lie black tangles of ruins. Nothing like that when I last was here. At Delancey Street an old Synagogue has become the Iglesa Adventista and on a tenement wall, four-stories high, blazes a great mural—VIVA PUERTO RICO LIBRE, a dawn in reds and yellows, Puerto Rican freedom fighters and Puerto Rican women, their laps filled with the rich harvest of the island. I see more Chinese. A beautiful red enameled perfectly restored Model-A Ford is parked outside a garage.

I ask myself what's different since I last walked on Forsyth Street and I know the answer. It is in me. I feel edgy. I walk more rapidly. I think I hear Puerto Rican youngsters huddled on a doorstep shout after me. It begins to drizzle. I am glad. Not likely anyone will come after me in rain. Why this feeling of tension? There's nothing on the street to arouse it. It's what I've read for the last ten years—that and my own absense from the

The Nativity Mission School brings light to the darkness of the old New York slum at 204 Forsyth Street, in the heart of the Lower East Side. (Courtesy, THE JESUIT)

Father Eugene Feeney, "Feen" as he likes to be called, and friend.
Father Feeney, a Jesuit, keeps the Nativity Mission School afloat.

streets. I'm no longer familiar with the unclear signs that spell safety and danger. Actually, Forsyth Street is as dreary, as drowsy, as quiet as I remember it. I almost walk past the six-story tenement at 204 with its faded white-painted sign then quickly duck into the entryway and pull open the door. This is the Nativity Mission School, Nativity Mission Center it was when I last was here, then run by two men of sinuous faith, two Jesuit priests, Father Walter Janer, who founded it, and his companion, Father John G. Hoodak, an island of light on a dark street.

I've come back because I think of Forsyth Street as a kind of monitoring station in the heart of the East Side, a slum as old, as desolate, as depraved as can be found in the land. I can take a reading and perhaps determine whether there is still hope for the greatest city of our America.

I find Father Feeney up three flights. His first name is Eugene and he hates it. People call him "Feen." He is fifty-one and speaks with the classic flat New York Irish voice, which is beginning to become rare. He worked eight years in Puerto Rico before getting his master's degree in urban affairs in St. Louis. He wears a gray checked shirt, dark trousers, a white-black-and-gray pullover and horned rim glasses. He chain smokes, has been running Nativity since 1970 and wears his clericals only to church and funerals. The year he came in, he transformed the Mission into a school. The mission has counseled hundreds of Puerto Rican families and youngsters on Forsyth Street, but it had gone about as far as it could go. By the time Father Feeney arrived youngsters had taken over the center. They were shooting up in the halls and selling beer in the basement to bankroll dope operations. It was nothing to find needles in the sinks and parties ran until 1 A.M. and 2 A.M.

One day one of the kids was shot and killed in a bowling alley on Fourteenth Street by some Chinese. It was a dope killing. A mission youngster had been peddling bad drugs. By mistake the Chinese shot the wrong boy (the guilty one has never been seen again). Father Feeney went to the funeral. It was held out on the island somewhere on the border of Queens and Brooklyn. There were forty cars in the procession. When they started to lower the coffin, the youngsters shouted: "Don't worry Kiki. We'll get him for you. We'll get him." Father Feeney commented: "Let's let the cops get him." When the coffin rested in the grave, a youngster said "that son-of-a-bitch funeral director is going to grab the coffin." The kids took up shovels and filled Kiki's grave until it was four or five feet above the ground. But, said Father Feeney, they hadn't been back in the car twenty minutes on the way to New York before they were talking about that night's dance as though nothing had happened.

"That was when I decided to change the mission into a school," Father Feeney said. "After all education is what we Jesuits are supposed to be good at."

When I last came to Forsyth Street, Father Janer told me that there was a large drug-cutting factory in the neighborhood as well as pushing on the street. So far as Father Feeney knows there's no drug factory any more. But Sara Roosevelt Park has become one of the biggest retail drug drops in the city. The location moves about the neighborhood a bit but it never closes. As in Father Janer's day the kids are the pushers. They get hooked in the late years of grade school and sell dope to support their habit. They call the Park Junkie Stadium. When there was talk of moving Yankee Stadium to Hackensack, the pushers became alarmed. People told them: "They're moving the stadium to Hackensack." "My God," the kids said. "What are we going to do—we don't know how to get to Hackensack."

Father Feeney's school is small. Five young men and Feeney run it. Two teachers are former Jesuits who had been working in the mission until they left the order to get married. They go on teaching at one hundred dollars a week, but how long that can continue, Father Feeney wonders. Four men live at 204 Forsyth, Father Feeney, two priests and Mike Mincielo, principal of the school and Father Feeney's right-hand man. Mike has been on Forsyth Street since he got out of Fordham in 1961. They know every crack in the sidewalk, every broken window on Forsyth Street. They walk in safety, the only danger that of a derelict panhandling for a quarter.

Nativity is an eight-grade school. This year it has thirty-seven kids although it would like to have fifty. The classes are small, never more than fifteen or sixteen, sometimes as small as four. Every youngster comes off the pavement of Forsyth or a nearby street, most of them out of PS 20. Ed Durkin, a young Jesuit, selects most of the candidates. He looks them over in school, talks to their teachers and classmates, goes to their homes. He's not searching out academic excellence. There is no such thing on Forsyth Street. He is looking for potential, youngsters who have ability but think they haven't, ones that have a decent chance of being lifted out of the slum. The idea is to give the youngsters and their families some marks to shoot at, a chance to work their way out of poverty toward the middle class.

"This is no big deal," Father Feeney says. "We know we are just a small drop in a big pond. But that is one reason why we can do the thing we do. We think that we have a partial answer to the problems of the street. That answer is education. It gives a few kids in the slum a means of getting out of the neighborhood. We expand their horizons for them. You have to remember the range of choices in the neighborhood is very limited."

I remember that from the days of Father Janer and from my long talks with the teen-age gang kids. Most of them had two goals in life, either to become a cop (because cops "have it made. They can do what they like legally") or to become an adult gangster. Most of them never made either. They were dead or in prison before they were out of their teens.

Father Feeney is trying to give the youngsters goals they can attain and a sense of social concern. "We have to transform them," he said. "We owe them something and they must feel like helping the others."

The first time Father Feeney invited the parents in for a meeting, there was a terrific blizzard and *West Side Story*, the Puerto Rican classic, was shown on TV. All but one parent showed up. It's been the same since.

A growing number of youngsters come from the Dominican Republic. The Dominican families are not on relief. They have to make it on their jobs. They work hard. So do their children.

When I met Father Janer, Nativity Mission ran on a budget of $18,000, which he raised personally in nickels, quarters and dollar bills. It still costs virtually nothing. The Father Provincial provides $17,500, and Father Feeney matches that. "I have some well-to-do friends," he says. "Along toward the end of the year as it gets toward income-tax time, I get some donations."

I leave 204 Forsyth and walk up to Houston Street. A man is urinating against a building. A garbage can has been spilled at the entrance to Sara Roosevelt Park beside a stripped red Pontiac. Two girls are hustling the cars coming by in a steady traffic flow.

As I walked out of 204 Forsyth, I noticed a small sign tacked on the wall: IF ANYONE SAYS I LOVE GOD YET HATES HIS BROTHER, HE IS A LIAR.

I take the subway back uptown. The city may be a jungle to some, but the beacon still burns. Our arms are still outspread to the poor and the downtrodden. With men like Father Feeney, with the tradition of Father Janer, with dedication to those great generations of New Yorkers whose social conscience fired the world, I believe New York and the other great cities of our country will find their way forward again. The light on Forsyth Street may be a small one, but it gives a spark that stirs my heart.

There is probably no better place than a schoolroom to judge of the character of a people.

—*Francis J. Grund, 1837*

I HAD BEGUN TO MOVE about the schools and colleges. This was where the great upheavals of the 1960s had been centered and it had been the young who had shown the way.

Now the young were said to be placid, quiet, hewing to their studies, worrying about jobs, bored with Washington and Watergate. People had begun to compare them with the students of the Fifties. I remembered in those days asking a young man at Princeton to characterize the mood of the campus. "Indifferent!" he said with such feeling that I did not ask another question.

I do not think that the Seventies are a rerun of the Fifties. A young man at Walla Walla College in Washington, a Vietnam veteran, was bothered that no one seemed interested in the war. It made him feel his years in Vietnam had been spent in a vacuum. Most of his classmates were looking ahead to their jobs. Walla Walla is a center of agribusiness. The fields of peas and vegetables are sold in advance to packers and harvested by them. Studeı ts do much of the work, riding the two-story cabs of the rigs all through the night, searchlights going. Coming down by plane the land looks like the surface of the moon. Huge circles are marked out on the flat floor of the valley—the limits of the walking irrigators, continuously moving sprays of water which slowly revolve on the dry desert land. The fields are no longer planted in rectangular swatches but in circles for irrigation nozzles. Harvest is a continuous process. The monster machines move through the fields, a parade of trucks following the fuming spouts.

"Sometimes," the youngster told me, "the truck is late or out of line. In a minute, two or three hundred pounds of peas spew onto the field."

But the machines move on. No one has time to heed the waste. It bothers the students who drive the monsters. They feel there is something wrong with such a mechanical world. They're not quite certain what is wrong but I think it's the fact the factory has come to the field with precision timing, no halt for spills that might feed a hundred families, onward to meet the production schedules set by computers. That is what bothers me. It reminds me of a scene from Kapek's R.U.R., the robots moving across the land, unseeing, unfeeling, remorseless.

In New Jersey a young instructor at Bergen college talks of the students of the Seventies. They are not as passionate as those of the Sixties. The campus is quiet. None of the presidential candidates seem interesting and economic considerations take over. But the atmosphere of the classroom has grown stimulating. This is because older persons are coming back to college, persons who have retired or persons who have lost their jobs or persons whose interests are changing in mid-life. The older students speak up. They have opinions on every subject. The youngsters feel challenged. The classroom springs to life.

This, I learn, is true across the country. At Fullerton, California, the oldest student is ninety. There is a heavy enrollment of forty-year-olds. Inevitably the college offers classes in "creative retirement" and instructs senior citizens on mortuary and cemetery rip-offs. But the heart of the spirit is the confrontation of the young and the old. For many it is the first time they have talked and argued across the bridge of the years.

One night in autumn I am sitting beside a young man in a heavy Chevy wagon rumbling through the Kentucky night down Highway 150 from Danville to Louisville. The blue grass, the miles of white board fences, the exquisite stables and the thoroughbreds are invisible in the dusk. Henry Welles, a student at Centre College, is driving me to the Executive Inn at

Louisville Airport and talking as though he will never stop. He is a sophomore and he comes from an almost classic Eastern affluent background, New York suburbs, parents writers in the great Luce empire, a wonderfully comfortable, exciting home. Henry is saying what is on his mind, what he has been thinking about for months or years.

He likes Kentucky and thinks he might even settle down here. It's a relaxed environment. But, my God, he exclaims, can you believe there are people in school who watch daytime television serials? Nothing, he believes, saps the imagination as does TV. Turns the mind into jelly.

"You were lucky," he says. "You grew up on radio. That extends your imagination."

There is a pause.

"You know," he resumes, "I was a Nixon supporter. Actually worked for him. I wouldn't believe Watergate. One day they called us together and asked for volunteers to help out at a breakfast meeting. Naturally I said yes. Then they said be sure to wear neat suits, jackets and ties, all that. I thought that was kind of funny and when we arrived, it turned out we were being used as an example, to demonstrate that nice young people with the right kind of haircuts and suits and ties were still supporting the President."

"Then came the tapes," he said. "And all the rest. You don't know how that made me feel."

"I guess," I said, "that you felt you'd been used."

"Right," he said. "Betrayed." It felt terrible and he can't get over it.

"Sometimes," he said, "I read Lincoln at night, the Gettysburg Address, and I get choked up. I have a tape of President Kennedy. I can't play it without crying."

He felt so bad he began to think he ought to join the Socialist Party or the Communist Party.

"Don't do that," I said.

He agreed.

"But," he said, "you don't know how terrible it is. I'm only nineteen and what is there to believe in?"

He didn't think much of any of the candidates, Republican or Democratic.

"I just don't have faith in anything," he said. "You people of the thirties were lucky."

"Why?"

"Well, times were bad but you had faith. You weren't disillusioned. You believed that things would come out all right in the end."

"That's right," I said softly, "that's right."

But was it? I sat thinking as Kentucky rolled past in the murk. Faith . . . things will come out all right . . . *Really?*

Is that what we had? I remembered living newly married in a cement-floored "English basement" on Chicago's Near North Side. My pay was thirty dollars until it was cut to twenty seven dollars. I was lucky. Most of my friends had no jobs. There was no relief, no unemployment insurance.

Did we have faith it was all coming out okay? I remembered my friend Reuben Cohen. We had gone to school together. His father escaped from Russia to avoid conscription. Now Reuben was a Communist and had changed his name to Robert Curtis.

"Why did you do that, Reuben," I asked him.

"Because of the pogrom. It's bound to come with the Fascists. I suppose they'll find out I'm a Jew, but I'll tell them I'm a wop. Maybe I'll get by. No use advertising I'm a Jew."

He took me to my first big demonstration. It was on Michigan Avenue in front of the Tribune Tower, directed against the Japanese invasion of Manchuria. Why was it held in front of the Tribune Tower? Could Colonel McCormick have been supporting the Japanese—not likely. The street was jammed. Suddenly I heard a small pop, like the pop of a snapper we pulled at children's parties. It was a revolver shot. Chicago's mounted police plowed into the mass, nightsticks flailing. People fell under the rearing horses and I ran for safety. It would be two generations before I would run again from the Chicago police, not until the Convention of 1968, but the sensation of sickly panic would not change.

Faith . . . Did I have faith that afternoon in February, 1933, when I boarded the New York Central train in Chicago and set off for Detroit with my uncle's alligator gladstone filled with rolls of nickels, dimes, quarters and half-dollars? I was a reporter in U.P.I.'s Chicago bureau, and this was money to keep our Detroit bureau going, money for phones, taxicabs, cigarettes and needle beer. The Detroit banks were closed and a few days later they closed all over the country.

Did I have faith as I slumped in my $3.75 coach seat, eyes on the window, watching the countryside go by, moving nearer and nearer to Detroit, not a feather of smoke rising from the great auto plants? Chrysler was dead. So was GM. So was the

Ford Dearborn works, the greatest of them all. All locked and shut behind high wire barricades and along the Detroit River miles and miles of lean-tos and shacks, tin-can towns, caves hollowed out of the clay sides of the river banks. Shantytown U.S.A. Smoke rose from hundreds of campfires, from tin-can kettles and mulligan stews. The glow of the campfires was amber in the dusk and it silhouetted the hulks of the great factories. Dead. Devastated. In my notebook I jotted a young reporter's impressions. I was getting in on the apocalypse of the American dream. Never again, I wrote, would smoke pour from the tall stacks of River Rouge. It was not everyday that you watched the swan song of the dinosaurs.

What a great dream it had been, I thought, and now it was gone. I had no idea of what might come, but the future would be exciting. I had a ringside seat for the death of the old and the birth of the new.

Next morning I went down to City Hall to talk to Detroit's radical young mayor, Frank Murphy. His office was in the open in the center of City Hall behind a mahogany railing. Four or five men arrived. I knew they were important by their dress. Large men, dignified. One, I believe, carried a gold-headed cane.

Murphy rose to meet them with a smile, trying to make them more comfortable but they were beyond comfort. These were the men whose hands had been at the throttle. They were the bankers and they had come for help. I could not hear their words, but I could see their lips quiver and one broke into tears. Murphy shyly put an arm around his shoulder. There was nothing he could do but speak a few warm Irish words. No one could help. Murphy knew it, the bankers knew it.

I turned back to Henry Welles. How could I tell him all of that. How could I tell him what it had *really* been like to discover your father was borrowing money from the loan sharks and taking his gold watch and cufflinks to a pawnshop?

Had we kept our faith? I suppose in an inverse way we had. We knew that the old system had crashed and that we would build a new one that was bound to be better.

We were coming up on Louisville now, the landscape filled with the trashy lights of the motels and franchisers. Yes, I guess I could understand why the 1930s were beginning to look like an American Dunkirk when we had all stood together. It was a myth but perhaps the strength of the American legend was in such myths.

8

The United States, of course, was born in political violence.
—STAFF REPORT TO NATIONAL COMMISSION ON VIOLENCE, *1970*

I AM SITTING IN THE living room of Hunter Thompson's ranch house, Woody Creek, on a spine of the foothills about eight miles from Aspen. Outside there is a steady fall of snow. Within there's a big blaze in the fieldstone fireplace and Juan, the Thompsons' eight-year-old, climbs over a low redwood table to put more logs on. Everything is confusion. I arrived with a TV crew and we've spent the whole day to put a half hour on tape. Beyond the picture window two peacocks preen themselves under a Plexiglas screen that protects them from snow. Inside, the electricians tease the Mina bird, which keeps repeating: "Mina birds can't talk." The Doberman bounces in and out of the house. I don't know how Hunter's wife, Sandy, with her long blonde hair and blue sweater, keeps her mind.

I'd come to see Hunter because it seemed to me that of all of those on the leading edge of the 1960s he was farthest out. No one had captured the random violence, the alienation of America as he had in *Hell's Angels* and *Fear and Loathing in Las Vegas.* If anyone could sense where the Seventies were heading, where things were beginning to happen, it should be Hunter.

Hunter had been uptight about our conversation. "I thought you were going to be very heavy," he said later. He bounded out of his bedroom in the morning to find the kitchen filled with technicians. "My God!" he exclaimed. "I didn't know you were all here." He plunged for his dark glasses, fitted them to his eyes, picked up a quart bottle of orange juice and downed most of it. What he really prefers in the morning is grapefruit.

The National Basketball Tournament is on and Hunter must go to Aspen to watch Kentucky play Maryland before we start talking. He wants to see the game with his Aspen chums. They like to bet and Hunter is certain Kentucky will win. He returns angry. "I'm not going to switch on NBC anymore," he says. "The bastards cost me four hundred dollars." They hadn't broadcast the Kentucky game.

"Yes," he says, "I'm very strong on betting. There's one thing—bets have to be paid. And reporters don't pay their bets." He made me feel a little guilty.

While I waited for Hunter to come back from the basketball broadcast, I wandered around his house. He had notes and souvenirs tacked up on the kitchen walls—Impeach Nixon posters, letters from Nixon types and transportation bills from the White House (relics of his campaign coverage). There was also the Anthony Lukas spoof in *More,* a fantasy scene in which Hunter bops a bartender to the floor and carves: "The American Dream" on his chest with a shard from the bottle. The spoof was so realistic that until Lukas ran a disclaimer reporters on the George McGovern campaign had given Hunter strange looks and shunned his company.

Hunter likes to project an image of violence and has since he lived with the Hell's Angels bikers, gathering material for his book and nearly getting beaten to death in the process. He tells me he's been warned by doctors that he's too violent to use LSD and that his tension level is so high that "I'll either melt or explode."

When he was living with Hell's Angels, however, there came a night when he introduced them to Ken Kesey. It was such a horrible scene he thought: "Well if I'm going to take this stuff I might as well do it now because I'm not going to live through this night anyway."

In the morning he experienced great relief. He had done nothing weird. And he was alive. Finally he got to the point where he could get a head full of acid and drive his motorbike across the Bay bridge, the bridge looking like a golden ribbon

Hunter Thompson, the gonzo journalist of Rolling Stone, *believes we are "totally doomed," but has great faith in the perversity of people. He is seen here with the author during a television interview.*

across the sky as he drove at one hundred twenty miles an hour, wearing shorts, no glasses and a tee shirt.

"I was really pushing myself," he says, "going about as far as you can without totally destroying yourself."

Did Hunter actually drive across the bridge, his head full of acid at 120 miles an hour? I'm not sure.

"It's been one of your problems, Hunter, hasn't it that people don't understand when you're putting them on," I say.

"Yeah," replies Hunter. "It has been a lot longer than most people realize, I think. Maybe even longer than I realize. I'm not even sure myself anymore."

Hell's Angels, he feels, is not just about the gangs.

"It's about this country," he says. "About those people

who had the leading edge, the most bizarre and the most obvious and shameless edge of what even then was creating a useless class. Musical chairs was going on and technology was beating them [the Angels] out of their chairs."

Now, he says, what with the economic situation there will be a lot more random violence.

"They won't all wear the colors of say, the Hell's Angels," he said. "They may wear: Da Nang '68, or Cameron Bay '69. I think we're going to have a very nasty backlash."

This, I suppose, is what Bly calls that lump in the belly, Vietnam.

Thompson has deep sympathy for the outcasts of society. He thinks of himself as an outcast symbol. When your options are down to zero and the only way of getting money is taking it from someone, he understands what happens. He thinks he would do it himself. I say there is not much difference between the Hell's Angels and the teen-age bopping gangs I got to know on the streets of New York at the end of the fifties except perhaps in age and technology. Both are discards of a society which has neither need of nor interest in them. Hunter agrees.

He never regarded himself as a spokesman for the drug culture, although that was where he lived in the mid-Sixties in San Francisco.

"I happen to be a person who does most things to excess," he says, "and so it would just be normal that I'd do it with drugs. I've learned a lot and maybe I've burned my mind out, maybe I've gone crazy, maybe I've destroyed myself but that doesn't worry me too much right now."

Hunter boils with nervous energy. He smokes a dozen cigarettes, then switches to small black cigars. He takes snuff two or three times as we sit talking on the big davenport. He jumps up for a beer and then gets out his favorite Wild Turkey, which he keeps on ice in a half-gallon bottle.

We talk on but we never get very far from violence. It hangs in the air and in Hunter's mind. When he was with the Angels he saw a kind of violence he never knew existed— people who really wanted to hurt other people. But no one can live for long like that. He is afraid the United States has that image, swaggering about the world, rattling sabers and threatening violence. He has learned from politics that you never make threats unless you are capable of carrying them out, intend to carry them out, and people know you will.

That is where Hunter has come to—politics. The Chicago convention, with its blind rage turned him in that direction. He came back to Colorado and ran for office himself, ran for sheriff and came within six votes of election.

"There's a high in politics," he says. "It's a combination of power and adrenaline which beats any drug I've found yet. Yeah. When its not fun you stop."

He's obsessed with the feeling of time running out. He is getting older. He never expected to live to be twenty. He was astounded when he reached thirty and he is baffled at the idea that he probably will live to be forty.

"You know," he says, "I hadn't planned on that."

He sees politics as the alternative to violence.

I notice Oswald Spengler's *Decline of the West* on his bookshelf. I wonder whether that's what he is into. Many people think Hunter personifies our disintegrating culture. But he is only marginally interested in Spengler, more or less as an insurance policy. If the West is declining, he should know about it. Perhaps, it is declining in the sense of some other civilization rising to replace it. After all the American experiment is very short-lived.

"We haven't been here long enough even to call ourselves a civilization," he adds.

Hunter can hardly wait to get into the 1976 Presidential campaign. He has a favorite—Georgia's Jimmy Carter. He's taped two speeches of Carter's and now he puts the tapes on his three thousand dollar electronic system and the soft Georgia voice shakes the walls of the big living room.

Carter is talking about education and what he says makes good sense. He is not afraid to come on as an intellectual to a hometown Georgia audience. Hunter has a date to meet Carter in Atlanta the next day and go to the stock-car races, but the snow falls more and more heavily. No planes are going to get out of Aspen on this night. Sandy gets on the telephone, trying to revise Hunter's travel arrangements. It's complicated and I can see it's not going to work.

Hunter is relaxed now. He wants me to see his study in the basement, a writing vault to which no sound penetrates. I don't know how much writing he does there. Hunter cannot really work unless he is on the edge of a deadline. He works best when he is past his deadline. I mention his fixation, the feeling that time is always running out. Right, he says and leads me over to his typewriter. Look what I've got pasted up over the machine. I look. We both look. There is nothing there. Christ, Hunter says, I must have torn it down. It was a clipping saying "Time is running out." There are guns all over the walls of

Hunter's study, submachine guns, pistols, heavy hunting rifles. They don't look as though they are used. There is also a sleeping bag on the floor and his election campaign poster with a stylized marijuana flower as its symbol.

Hunter muses about the world. He makes mistakes but he has no guilt feelings. The world is pretty rough and if you are going to hurt people, even by accident, you might as well hurt the right ones.

Hunter has read a book put out by the University of Virginia Press. Conversations with William Faulkner when he was writer in residence there.

"This is no bull," he said, "It really said what I think about the fate of man. You know when the last bomb goes off and the last cypress tree falls in the last mud bog there'll still be some, you know, weak, ugly, human voice saying, wait a minute, I'm here. I don't know—it's still in my interest to believe that right now. And that we're totally doomed, which I do on one level. But I think there's a perversity in people that I kind of like and have great faith in."

So there it all hangs out. Hunter Thompson, the man of doom, the cutting edge of the out culture of the 1960s is an optimist on the survival of humanity.

It's been a good talk and Hunter and I think of meeting again in New York or possibly on the campaign trail. Back at the motel his preoccupation with violence echoes in my mind. This is a deep American strain and he is right, I think, to draw the equation between violence in American life and the violence in her relations with the world. We *are* a violent people and we have been from the early days. This is what is easy to miss along the path of emigration and the movement to the West. There are traces of it in Hiram's diary but only traces—the murders, the killings, the rapes. This was what lay in the background of Bly's remarks about the killings in Vietnam and the killings at home, the massacre of the Indians, which after so many years has come back to haunt us.

I remember the staff report to the President's National Commission on the Causes and Prevention of Violence, the great study Johnson had ordered after the assassinations of John Kennedy, Martin Luther King, Robert Kennedy, Malcolm X, George Rockwell, the Yablonskis (the attempt on George Wallace's life had not yet been made).

There were the words of the report:

"Violence had been used by successive generations of na-

tive Americans [primarily white Anglo-Saxon Protestants] to oppose a perceived cultural, economic, social and moral threat
posed by successive waves of immigrants from Catholic and
non-Teutonic Europe, and to reinforce the moral values of fund-
amentalist Protestantism."

We had used the gun to drive the Indians from the lands
we seized. We used the gun and the rope to terrorize the blacks.
The American dream had been a bloody dream. Our nation had
been born in political violence and racial violence. I grew up to
the refrain: The only good Indian was a dead Indian. The only
Indians I saw were harmless drunks around the Union Station.
But the deadly echo of pioneer warfare lingered on in our folk-
ways. The dark stain was there and Hunter's words would not
let me forget it.

I am sitting in the cafe of the Ritz-Carlton in Boston with
Priscilla McMillan. I've known Priscilla since the days when
we chanced to occupy next-door rooms at the Metropol Hotel in
Moscow and I've sought her out to talk once more about the
assassination of John F. Kennedy, a subject to which she has
devoted more than a decade of her life.

As I travel around the country, one theme comes up again
and again in my conversations. It is not Richard Nixon nor
Watergate. I am surprised how rarely these names are mentioned. But there is hardly a conversation which does not ulti-
mately turn to Kennedy, Dallas, Martin Luther King, Bobby and
all that has followed.

I find in the consciousness of Americans, young, old,
middle-aged, white, black, north, south, east or west an aware-
ness, a persistence, a preoccupation with violence and conspiracy, which stems from the events in Dallas of November 22,
1963, and which does not diminish with the years.

Dallas has left its mark on each of us. I bear its mark as
well. From the moment when, as I sat at the long table in the
third-floor dining room of the Century Association on Forty-
Third Street and a member in solemn tones (I can hear them
now) told us: "Gentlemen, I am very sorry to say it but President Kennedy has been shot in Dallas" it has been part of my
life. I left the table before the words were completely out of
Alfred De Liagre's mouth and ran two and a half blocks down
Forty-third Street to *The New York Times*, where I took over
direction of covering the Kennedy story.

For months and years the tragedy played a central role in

my professional life, and I do not expect to see the end of its permutations. Nor has this come as a surprise. On the morning after Kennedy died, I wrote in my notebook that one hundred years from that date, November 23, 1963, the controversy over Kennedy's death would still rage. Nor did this take great presence of mind. As a young newspaperman in Chicago each year on the anniversary of Lincoln's assassination, I had written a story about some new theory of his death, some new conspiratorial thesis, some new "evidence" belatedly disclosing that Lincoln did not, in fact, die of the shooting at the Ford Theater that night in Washington in the manner history recorded.

I had long since arrived at my own conclusion why the official version of Kennedy's death was so universally rejected—for the rejection was universal. As I traveled the world I found few in Paris or London who believed either the initial reports or the findings of the Warren Commission. It was the same in Asia. I had argued the case in Sikkim in the Himalayas and in a jeep en route to the Gobi Desert in Mongolia. I never met anyone in Russia who believed Kennedy died in the way I believed he died. Certainly Khrushchev didn't. Nor did Brezhnev. Nor my poet friends, Andrei Voznesensky and Yevgeny Yevtushenko.

In peasant huts in Siberia I had seen Kennedy's photograph still gracing the walls, like a modern ikon, and I had heard Siberians confidently confide that they "know all about these assassinations." Well, they had a point. In Russia assassination had *always* been the product of conspiracies. That was true in the day of the Czars and in the plots against Lenin's life by the Socialist Revolutionaries. And often, as in the death of Sergei Kirov, the Leningrad leader who was killed December 1, 1934 (an event used by Stalin to touch off the Great Purges), the complicity of the police was evident.

I never attempted to convince a Russian that Kennedy was killed by one man, acting on his own, a loner, an outcast of society named Lee Harvey Oswald. Nor did I argue with those I met on my travels about America who again and again told me of their conviction that President Kennedy, Robert Kennedy, Martin Luther King and the others were the victims of a gigantic conspiracy in which the CIA, the FBI and/or the Cuban government had a role.

Why argue? Reason and logic were not going to change anyone's mind, and I had reluctantly come to the view that the revelations of Watergate, the White House and the CIA had exposed so many bizarre and unbelievable actions that the deepest suspicion of the "conspiracy" buffs seemed quite ordinary. Even sensible.

It was wrong, I thought, to describe the country as being in a state of paranoia. To the contrary—the men and women with whom I talked were merely drawing sensible conclusions based on norms of conduct which had been disclosed as having been practiced in Washington in recent years.

There was another reason why we found it so hard to accept the idea that Kennedy had been shot by a simple neurosis-ridden man named Oswald. This explanation was emotionally unacceptable and psychologically repulsive. So great a man, a hero like Kennedy, a hero-king as it were, a man in shining armor could not suffer so lowly a death. Our minds rejected the idea that a great man could be brought down by so trivial a figure. We told ourselves it simply *couldn't* happen that way. The bright hero could not fall to Oswald's bullet. His grandeur cried for a death which was consistent—a plot of enormous complexity, of demon powers capable of blotting out the Sun King.

I did not know what psychologists might make of my idea, but I had seen the syndrome in people's thinking. The emotional basis for it was laid long before the publication of the Warren report, with its dry, detailed commonplace conclusions. It died away a bit after the Warren report only to sweep forward anew like a great epidemic. Now it had become chronic and periodically seized us like ague in a malaria patient, wracking our bodies and making our minds numb.

This was what I had encountered in my travels about America and I wanted to touch base again with Priscilla McMillan whose long, long inquiry into the Dallas events was finally drawing toward a conclusion as was her husband's parallel inquiry into the assassination of Martin Luther King.

Once again I asked Priscilla: Why Dallas? Why had Kennedy met his death in this Texas city? At that time Dallas had radiated hate, violence and intolerance. It reminded me not a little of the climate which had gripped Birmingham at the opening of the decade of the 1960s. The atmosphere had been so tense in Dallas that my first instinct (and that of many others) was to suspect some concatenation of evil forces, some conspiracy of democracy haters. Like others I had been reluctant to abandon that notion—dropping it only in the end after the painstaking Warren inquiry supported what the independent inquiry, which I directed for *The Times*, had already made clear that, in fact, Oswald was a loner, a loner among loners.

But what did Priscilla think after the years of digging, after spending a year of her life actually living with Marina Oswald, after talking to all those who were close to the case, after sifting the great volumes of the Warren report and the endless tomes of the anti-Warren conspiratorial buffs—was there any special reason why Kennedy was killed in Dallas? Had that atmosphere of hate and violence made any contribution?

She did not think so. It had happened in Dallas because Oswald happened to be in Dallas. True, the atmosphere had been turgid. But this did not really affect Oswald. He was too isolated from it. Could the killing have happened in New Orleans or in the North? Priscilla thought so. The atmosphere which surrounded Oswald was charged with hatred and violence. Yet, Oswald lived so much within himself. He was not necessarily stimulated by right-wing propaganda, by hate literature, by any of the things that were going on around him.

To Priscilla the trigger was to be found in the inner tensions of Oswald's life, his relations with Marina, sexual taunts, the dark psychology of Oswald's haunted mind.

I looked about the decorous cafe, the careful expressions on the faces of the stylish young Boston women, the serious Bostonian men with their luncheon talk of investment opportunities and low-risk high-yield securities. Not a hint here of the turbulence that had fed into America's bloodstream in the years that had followed Kennedy's death.

But the virus was in our minds. It circulated there, mixing with the poison of events which had followed. Small wonder that I heard again and again from quiet men and women in the byways of their feeling that "there's something wrong," that "we don't know all the things that have happened."

I thought of all that *had* happened in the dozen years since Kennedy's death, the ravages of Vietnam, the boiling up of the colleges and universities, the fire and guns in the ghettoes, the suspicion, the taint, the hypocrisy, the fears of Washington.

How many years before we purged ourselves of the ravages of hatred and suspicion? Many years. Not in my lifetime. Nor, I thought, would Priscilla's cool, logical compelling words cure the latent paranoia which now seized us all.

In the end only time would do the job completely, the passage of time and the dimming of the fresh pain of our recollections. Time and the painstaking reexamination of our national ethos, which had now been underway for nearly a quarter of a century. Only when we had faced up publicly and totally to the shameful image of our own reality would we be able once again to face the future joyfully and realistically as in Hiram's day.

THE FIRST TIME I met Daniel Ellsberg his name meant nothing to me. Chance had brought us together in an academic seminar which was exploring how some of the decisions in Vietnam had been made. He was one of several young Washington bureaucrats and ex-bureaucrats who were trying to fit the pieces together. I was amazed by the things I heard. So far as those present could recall no specialist in Vietnam culture, history or philosophy had given testimony during the sessions at which the bombing of the North was being considered in Johnson's day. No one had raised a question, so far as the group could remember, of the possibility that bombing might not produce the desired end, Hanoi's surrender. No one mentioned the survey of strategic bombing carried out at the close of World War II demonstrating that bombing had been counterproductive, had strengthened Germany's will to resist and that her output of arms, oil, machinery and steel had actually *increased* under the rain of Allied bombs. It was a unanimous presumption that American bombing would automatically produce whatever result was desired. I remembered Ellsberg as a dark, intense, sardonic figure. After the Pentagon Papers broke a year or two later, I often recalled that discussion and Ellsberg's part in it. I had seen him occasionally since then and I wanted to get his thinking on where the country was headed now that Vietnam, in a manner of speaking, was behind us. I wondered whether he shared Bly's theory that Vietnam was a lump in our belly.

It is not easy to find Ellsberg nor is it easy to steer a

conversation away from the concerns which are uppermost in his mind. He lived then in Mill Valley, twenty minutes from San Francisco, a sunny suburban town that reminded me of Libertyville, north of Chicago, where Adlai Stevenson lived, or Darien, Connecticut—a town of healthy children, tennis-playing matrons, station wagons, Irish setters, English-timbered eating nooks and money. Lots of money. I followed my directions through town to a mountain road along a stream, narrow and stony and finally came to an end at a heavy redwood gate, weighed down with chains and locks. It looked as though I had gone as far as I was going to go. As I puzzled over the situation a mailman turned up in his car. Yes, he said, this is Ellsberg's gate, but the place is further up the mountain. He went over and pulled at the heavy chain. It came free in his hand. I pushed the gate open and eased my yellow Pinto to the top of the mountain, around a hairpin turn, up to a redwood house with large plate-glass windows. Birdseed had been scattered about the terrace, and inside I found Dan Ellsberg and my old friend Neil Sheehan, *The New York Times* reporter, talking.

Two tape recorders were going, Neil's and Dan's. The remains of several of Neil's big cigars rested in an ashtray and standing on the long redwood table was a brown flowered Japanese teapot and two bile-colored mugs. There was a rubbing over the brick fireplace, probably from Angkor, an Indian print on the wall and a jar of Blakely ginger marmalade beside the teapot.

Dan was talking about American foreign policy in the period after World War II and how, in his belief, it had been run by elitists who honestly felt that unless they took on this responsibility the ignorant politicians, the McCarthys and his equivalents, would conduct a more dangerous policy that would threaten real nuclear confrontation. Americans, he believed, thought of themselves as simple nationalists as we had been when our Republic came into the world and we wanted to support other nationalist movements. That came out of World War II. This had been Roosevelt's idea. But we never seemed to be able to back genuine nationalist movements, Betincourt and men like that, because we lacked confidence that they would support us when the chips were down. In the end, the ones we supported were right-wing dictators who could be depended on to oppose the Communists to the bitter end. These dictators were quite ready to take our aid and in return protect our sources of raw materials and our markets.

Dan Ellsberg gave history a shove by exposing the Pentagon Papers, and no one yet can say what the final consequences of his act will be. (Courtesy, THE NEW YORK TIMES)

In other words, he said, better a Trujillo than a Castro. He cited Dean Rusk as a prime elitist. I suggested that Rusk was not an elitist to my way of thinking. How about Mac Bundy? He persisted in his feeling that Rusk was one of the strongest among those who felt the country had to be protected against the mob and the mob's foreign policy. Ellsberg felt we wouldn't let real nationalists come to the top because they would threaten our markets and our resources. We could not get it through our heads that even if we did get "good nationalists" on our side, men who were not just crooks and grafters, in the end they were forced to become our patsies. This had happened in Vietnam.

Turning back to the war (and he never really got away from it), he did not believe that Rusk or Johnson or anyone really wanted to prolong the war for war's sake. But they did not want to end it on anything other than a victory.

I watched the birds fly down and scatter the birdseed over the terrace. There were Japanese wind chimes outside and they tinkled pleasantly in the wind. Finally, Neil picked up his notes and tape recorder and left. Dan had been walking around the house barefooted. Now he put on sandals and we rode down to Mill Valley in his Triumph Spitfire for a sandwich. He was alone in his house.

I had heard that Ellsberg had been moving toward a Marxian interpretation of politics and this seemed to be reflected in his discussion of the emerging nationalist movements.

Ellsberg bounded out of the TR to open the gate, bounded to the mailbox to get his mail and bounded back to the car. When we got to Mill Valley, he leaped from the car and ran up the steps of the grocery store, then ran back.

"You're quite a runner," I said. He agreed. He said he ran three or four miles a day and had done it for years. I could believe this. His compact body was all muscle and sinew.

Now we were back on Vietnam and LBJ. We talked of Johnson's speech of March 31, 1972, the partial bombing halt and his pull out of the race for reelection. I said I thought that Johnson was playing things in two directions. He hoped that Hanoi would reject his offer and that demand would arise that he seek reelection. I recalled that LBJ signs that had been found stashed in the Chicago stadium and the birthday party Mayor Daley had planned to hold for Johnson on the Sunday before the Democratic Convention. Hanoi's acceptance of Johnson's proposal, I said, was a surprise. At first Vietnam seemed on the point of rejecting it, then, possibly swayed by Johnson's refusal to seek reelection, they accepted it. There had been signs of confusion in the State Department and White House for several days, but they could find no way out of the dilemma. They couldn't say no to Hanoi's yes.

Ellsberg had some reservations about this theory, but what he was really interested in was why Nixon hadn't made peace soon after he came into office. Ellsberg had been called in by

Kissinger in the period after election when Nixon was in the Hotel Pierre in New York and drafted a questionaire on Vietnam under Kissinger's direction, submitting a 40,000-word summary of the responses. He called this document "Nixon #1" and said it provided a clear basis for going forward to a settlement. Then, the line had changed. What had changed it?

Ellsberg had a complicated theory. Nixon had given a speech in May, 1973, calling for a cease-fire. It sounded as though he was for peace. But actually Kissinger called in Soviet Ambassador Dobrynin and pointed to an obscure and threatening line and said that if Hanoi did not react positively, we were prepared to bomb Haiphong. Nixon's policy all along, Ellsberg thought, had been more hard-line than the public knew. On November 3, 1973, Nixon gave a public speech heralding a tough line on Vietnam. There had been speculation in Washington that it might be a soft-line speech. Actually, Ellsberg claimed, Nixon had been prepared to make a more hard-nosed speech, saying he was ready to bomb Hanoi and Haiphong and had been talked out of it at the last moment.

I could throw no light on that puzzle. We went back to the house and the talk continued to be all Vietnam. "I don't understand why I'm getting hoarse," he said drinking some cold tea. I knew he had talked most of the night before with Neil and had been talking all this day. His throat had to be sore.

What did Ellsberg see of the future? What could he see of the future? He was anchored in Vietnam, Bly's lump in the stomach. In fact, he was part of the lump. The telephone rang from time to time. Some Iranian students were going to demonstrate against the Shah. Ellsberg had a long talk about the details. He was going to Sacramento the next day. Fred Harris was having a rally. He rather liked Harris's populism. I think he felt it fitted his new efforts to find a Marxian key to the cataclysmic events in which he had been involved. Certainly he was not seeking answers in the old politics. He had been a man who at a decisive moment had literally wrenched events into a new course, not only the war but relations between the government and the people and the press and the establishment. We talked a bit about this. Why had the Nixon administration gone all out to suppress the Pentagon Papers, to enjoin the newspapers, to prosecute the newsmen and then, finally, in the full panoply of Nixon paranoia, to mount the plumbers' operation against himself, Ellsberg, which brought the whole pyramid crashing down? Why?

Charles Reich gave us our first understanding of youth in the 1960s in The Greening of America, *but he now seems distant from the mainstream. (Courtesy,* THE NEW YORK TIMES)

There was only one reason he could see. There must have been other things, probably things not yet exposed even after Watergate, which were going on and which Nixon feared might be disclosed. He hoped to use the Pentagon Papers to crush the press and clear the way to do as he pleased. Instead, he crushed himself.

I thought his hypothesis was sound and I wondered when, if ever, we would know the whole answer. I pondered over Ellsberg, as Hiram would have said, for a long time. I am still pondering. I am wondering whether Ellsberg's act in making public the Pentagon Papers has not set off a train of events whose consequences will run far, far into the future and in the end change our society more profoundly than we can now foresee. Without the Pentagon Papers I doubted that Watergate would have been exposed. And no one knew where this new path would lead. Bit by bit we were taking the structure of our society apart, examining the shoddy, shameful makings of it. Gradually we would put it all together again. But the shape and the substance would be different.

The longer I stayed in California the further I seemed to have left behind the pattern of America which I had traced from New England through New York and on to the heartland of Wisconsin, Minnesota and Iowa, the more distant seemed the image of the New England ethic and the Minnesota spirit.

It was almost as if the great barrier of the Rockies and sheer distance—never mind that it has been annihilated by jets and electronics—had created a different breed and a different culture.

I know that this is not true. San Francisco, at least, was founded by the same New England stock that opened the way to the heartland. But here there was a different rhythm. I felt this new cadence the moment I saw Charles Reich again.

Charles Reich is a man whom I immensely admire. He is a genuine American philosopher of his times. He was the first to grasp the scope of the youth rebellion of the 1960s. He ran it through his analytic mind and produced an almost poetic theory of what it meant. *The Greening of America* will be read for generations by those who are trying to understand what happened in that fateful decade. Reich's contribution was that he gave shape to what most of us had perceived as an inchoate mass. He related the explosion of the young to the structure of society and offered an interpretation founded on optimism.

I had, however, never quite agreed with Reich's ideas. It seemed to me that what began to happen in the late 1950s and continued through the 1970s was a step-by-step revolution in American institutions. Beginning with *Brown* v. *The Board of Education* and the civil-rights movement in the South (as Farrell Dobbs pointed out), we had in disorderly fashion, taken one American institution after the other, subjected it to battering criticism, and consolidated a series of new premises for American society.

At the bottom of all this lay that sense of alienation which I had found in my crisscrossing of the country, that inarticulate feeling that things had gone wrong; that the country was not what we had grown up supposing it was; that belief that it was not living up to the ideals of the forefathers; that, as Bly says, "the ministers lie, the professors lie, the television lies, the priests lie." The President had lied and Congress had lied and the newspapers had lied. Frustration had boiled up into one movement after another: the movement in the South; the movement in the colleges; the movement against the war; the movement for environment (against government and corporations); the movement for consumerism and Nader (against big business and government); the movement against Washington; against the media; against the White House; against New York City; for change in the church; against the CIA; against the young and against the old.

Always *against* something, something *big* and if the drive was stated in positive terms—*for* civil rights, *for* women's rights, black rights, Indian rights, homosexual rights—it was against the status quo.

I thought, in a word, that Reich's analysis in *Greening* was too limited but I thought, too, that it was a tour de force which had seldom been equalled.

Reich had left Yale, I knew, and come out to San Francisco. On one of those superlative San Francisco days with a fine wind whipping the sky clean of clouds, I found Reich in a wooden house in a row of wooden houses high over the city. I pushed the old bronze doorbell and he appeared, his dark leathery face lighting up, his hair longer and grayer than when I last saw him, wearing a white shirt with a neat embroidered band, dark duck trousers and tennis shoes. One tennis shoe was split at the rear because he has a broken Achilles tendon and must see the doctor once or twice a week.

Reich is a meticulous man. He revises and corrects and never is satisfied. His workroom was as meticulous as I had expected, his manuscript in careful compartments behind him, his desk precise and bare. It wasn't a cleaned-up room; it was the working place of a careful and exact man.

We went half a block along the street and up a flight of

steps to a terrace beside a cascade of shasta daisies, yellow nasturtiums, yellow roses, pink roses and purple and white flowers which I did not recognize. This was the home of a friend of Reich's, a warm dark-haired woman, and when we sat down she served one of the best lunches I have ever eaten— tomato stuffed with crab and shrimp, an artichoke, a quiche and strawberries in Devonshire cream. Beside the terrace grew a one-hundred-year-old sycamore. The house had been built just after the earthquake. After lunch we sat on big yellow cushions and talked.

I told Reich that I was an optimist. He was delighted. So were his friends. He said this was a time when the consciousness people of the 1960s were out doing their own thing (I give his thought as it remains in my memory, not in the precise terms he would employ himself). They are deliberately keeping their heads down, presenting a low profile. They are not success-oriented. They do work they like and some only work to earn enough to eat. He showed me two abstract paintings done by a blue-collar youth who works three months of the year on the assembly line and spends the rest of the time painting. When he runs out of money, he goes back to the assembly line. I didn't care for the abstracts, but I knew young people in the East and in the Midwest who followed a similar pattern, not dropouts from society but people who made the system work so they could lead a very personal kind of life.

What Reich liked about San Francisco was the growth of counterculture businesses, stores, restaurants, all run by people who were doing what they did because they enjoyed it. They were not thinking about money. Here was an example in which the new consciousness was actually changing society, without society's being aware of it.

Like me he dated the start of the big change to the civil-rights movement in the South. That evolved into the student movement of the 1960s. The students rampaged in the streets, broke windows, made headlines and got people mad at them. The present generation doesn't break windows and doesn't get into the headlines. People don't realize they are there.

I asked about himself. He had left Yale. For two years he had taught part-time, but he no longer could stand the atmosphere of the button-down-collar people. No new young people were coming into the law faculty. Here in San Francisco he could breathe, relax, make his own pace and lead his own life. But he did miss the students. He missed the feedback of bright, challenging minds. In San Francisco he lived with his own group, about a dozen people. Not a commune. Each was an individual, but all related to each other. They met and talked and spent their evenings together.

I wondered whether he thought the American system must undergo a structural change. Not in Reich's opinion. It can be changed by the people. The people know they have been lied to. They know that their Presidents have been crooks. They will compel change. The generation of new young Congressmen is evidence of this. There will be a President from the ranks of the consciousness people (as he calls the *Greening* generation) but not in the next election. Later.

For the time being, people are into ecology. They want to relate to the earth. They move counter to the directions set by big corporations and big institutions. They buy small cars. No matter what Detroit wants, they will do as they please. Society has become very individualistic. There is a respect for the individual and for individuality, a turning against uniformity.

And here he struck a note that brought it all together. This individuality he called the American theorem. This is what the emigrants came to America for. This was what Hiram was about and his ancestors and the whole New England tradition. Now this comes once more to the fore.

Reich speaks fervently. He trusts the people. Their wisdom is greater than that of their leaders. They know that they are right and the leaders are wrong. They are anti-leader. This underlies the anger of people at "politicians" and the success of candidates who present themselves as anti-politicians. It is not the system that is wrong, it is the crooked people in the system. He learned this lesson when he was a law clerk to Mr. Justice Clark.

Socialism—no, he sees no likelihood of a turn in that direction. But planning by government, yes. Just as big business plans so should government.

I expressed my skepticism of planning having seen its failure in the Soviet Union. Maybe, I said, it could work in Japan, where the government and business set goals together, but do we want business and government so closely intertwined?

He believes now that *The Greening of America* was a little premature. Consciousness existed among the young people, but not the knowledge of what to do with it.

I wonder about the rise of isolationism so many people talk of. He thinks this is nonsense. What we must do is solve our own problems and embark on a new and nondestructive foreign policy and stop imposing the American will on others. We must admit that this has not been the American century, which Henry Luce thought it would be.

He feels comfortable in San Francisco. It is a city which has not yet reached critical size. New York has become too big. Here the city is small enough for people to know each other and interact easily and naturally.

Education may be the new frontier. Many of the people of the Sixties have gone into education. They're in high schools, trade schools. There must be a revolution in education. Lots of the teachers do nothing but tranquilize the kids, hoping to keep them quiet in school.

He believes that women are the most important driving force in American society today. Marriages are in trouble. He doesn't know of a single marriage made in the Twenties, the Thirties, the Forties which is not in trouble.

Governor Brown interests him. He doesn't know whether Brown is liberal or conservative, but he is honest. He's a no-shit guy. He is the opposite of the royal myth of the White House. Lives in his old apartment and drives his own car. American liberals must get over the Presidential Palace psychology, Hail to the Chief, all that. He could go for Teddy Kennedy if he brought a lot of young kids into the White House, but he is still a member of the Old Establishment. They are all caught in the imperial trappings of the Palace.

We talk on in the warm San Francisco sunshine. Reich reads *The New York Times* every day. He misses his students and next year he will do a lot of lecturing in order to get back a sense of communication. This year he has been too busy working on his book.

He is impressed by the way the old life-style and the new life-style get along. They coexist peacefully in dress and manners.

Finally he comes back to the point basic to our discussion—the right of each person to create his own life and his own life-style. This is the American way. This is what the United States is all about and why it was created in the first place by people who had revolted against the pattern of living in their European homeland. They came to America to live life as they wanted, and if they did not like the pattern in the East or the Midwest they came in the end to California.

That was it, I thought, that is the special ingredient in

California life and psychology. There is a different pattern here and it is a blend of many individual strands, each spun by one individual who came here because he or she wanted "to get away."

Something troubles me about my conversation with Ellsberg and as I come away from talking with Reich I feel it again and try to understand what it is. It's not the conversations themselves, it is in the relationship of these two men to the march of national events. Each has played a role in a dramatic moment of history. They stood in what the Russians like to call the center and not the periphery; that is, they were connected with the great machinery which moves our society.

Today each lives in the paradisiacal setting of San Francisco, a city with which I fell in love in 1945, when I covered the founding conference of the United Nations. They are living lives which satisfy deep personal needs, Ellsberg in an eyrie at the end of a long twisting mountain road and Reich in a hideaway overlooking the white city. But they are not wired in to the action. They are at a remove from the thunderous course of events. They do not react and interact as they would in Washington or Yale. The *Times* arrives a day or two late. They do not meet their peers at lunch nor argue with them at cocktail time. The telephone does not replace talking it out face to face. Distance is not really annihilated. Perhaps, paradise is not the best place to dig for the elusive truth. Perhaps, the grit of New York, the cockpit of Washington, the tension of New England academia or the on-job experience of the young politicians in the heartland are better suited to keep minds sharpened to harsh realities. So it seems to me.

My conversation with Charles Reich is still running through my mind when I sit down with David Harris. Harris is a fighter against the Vietnam war. He tore up his draft card at Stanford in 1968, married Joan Baez two months later, went to prison for three years for his act of defiance and emerged from the Federal penitentiary in 1971. He and Baez were divorced in 1973.

Now Harris and Lacey Forsburgh, a writer and reporter, live in a house at the end of Stockton Street with a view of Golden Gate and Alcatraz that's like a giant picture postcard. For the first time in his life Harris has a job, working for *Rolling Stone*. Before that all his life had been in the movement against the war.

Harris has rusty sideburns and rusty long hair, a comfortable Scotch look and talks eloquently about his generation. As for himself he is into politics. He's running for the Democratic nomination for Congress in San Mateo Valley just to the south and he thinks he has a chance of winning. (He did—handily.) California, he believes, is becoming more radical, the blue-collar workers have lost confidence in the leaders and are ready to listen to a "long-haired war freak."

Harris is a third-generation Californian. His grandfather was a carpenter and there is something about Harris which suggests that he could be a good carpenter too if occasion arose. His generation cut its teeth in the civil-rights movement in the South. He went to Mississippi in the voter registration campaign of 1964. He would have gone in 1963 but couldn't get away. He had no fear of the consequences of going into the South and in that he was typical of his friends. Youngsters now, however, are more careful and don't put their heads up. They are job-oriented but he thinks this means they are just more prudent.

In his campaign he talks of sharing the means of distribution and other socialist ideas, but he does not use the word socialism because that is a dirty word to the voters. But he finds his ideas attractive to people. He is opposed to the kind of ideology which came up through SDS, the radical student movement. That was a time when everyone felt alone and was groping for something to bolster confidence, some kind of rationale to rally around and they found it in Marcuse even though they may not have read Marcuse very thoroughly. He remembers how they argued and argued about ideology and never got anywhere. He turned against it. Some stayed with it but no viable remnant of that movement remains alive.

Lacey brings up the women's movement as being still on the rise, a source of energy and importance. Harris disagreed. I sided with Lacey. It seemed to me there was more vitality in the women's movement than in most of the other inheritances of the 1960s.

We talked as does everyone in California about Governor Brown. Harris used much the same language about him as Reich—a no-nonsense, hard-nose approach, a political animal, not necessarily conservative, but the time would come when he had to face up to real problems and then he might be in trouble. Reagan, Harris said (and others echoed his thought) was no longer popular in California. The state had moved from him.

Not much was left of the radical movements. The Black Panthers were down the drain. The black radical movement had withered. The leaders had wandered away. Part of the problem was success. Any black female could get a job in California.

Haight-Ashbury had been dissolved by drugs. The flower children were no more. The current generation was much too wise. They didn't do things that were against the law.

To Harris the big thing was that Vietnam veterans were going into politics. They knew that Vietnam was a rip-off. Harris was running in Paul McCloskey's district. He considered McCloskey a true Republican except for the war issue.

Communes, he said, were thriving in California. Nearly all young people live in an extended group or cooperative, but they don't use the term commune. Harris doesn't like them because he doesn't like someone telling him what to do. But many people enjoy doing things in common. They talk together, share their income, live in one building or in communal apartments. No one pays any special attention anymore. They don't think of them as Communes with a capital C. People are living in groups back in the hills, squatters who are just let alone. People have accepted the new way of life. Hippies have vanished, just blended into the general culture.

Lots of young people don't go to college now. Bright kids see nothing there for them and want to do things with their hands. They have taken a lesson from the hippies and become carpenters or craftsmen. They don't meet opposition from their parents. The violent clashes of earlier days are over, possibly because the parents fear they will lose their children.

Harris talks of the war without passion until he gets to the subject of the Vietnam refugees. He is outraged that they are treated better than opponents of the draft. The draft evaders deserved a real amnesty and he's using this as a campaign issue.

California is a good state to campaign in because the atmosphere is permissive. There's not the kind of automatic opposition to new ideas you often encounter in the East.

Lacey teaches journalism at Stanford. She is struck by the idealism of her students. They give her a hard time on ethical questions. Not all the romanticism in journalism is the product of Woodward and Bernstein and the Watergate exposé. Lots of it stems from this new age of youth, skeptical about its institutions, challenging in its questions and sturdy in its ideals.

It seems to me that David Harris represents the first step by the young people of the 1960s to convert their struggle, their revolution if you will, into political power. It mortices into

Hunter Thompson and his fascination with politics. Harris is running a long-shot campaign in a single California district. But he is not alone in moving in this direction, nor is Minnesota the only state in which youth has entered the political ring. This strand in our national design seems to me to offer new promise.

One morning in 1965 I was sitting almost alone in the city room of *The New York Times* when a slight youngster appeared, looking a little like a puzzled rabbit, wearing khaki slacks and, I believe, tennis shoes. He had just come back from Hanoi and he wanted to talk to me about it.

Herbert Apteker, a well-known New York Marxist, and Stoughton Lynd, a Yale professor and peace leader, had been invited to North Vietnam. They wanted someone younger to make a third. Lynd knew a young radical named Tom Hayden and so Tom was invited to go along.

Now it is ten years later and Tom comes to see me at the Beverly Hilton in Los Angeles. He hasn't changed much, the same look of a rumpled youngster just in from the tennis courts, khaki slacks, open collar shirt. He is, I know, now running for nomination for the Senate seat held by Tunney.

I had met Tom occasionally in the years between 1965 and 1975. Wherever the Movement of the 1960s went Tom was to be found—the South, Hanoi, Chicago, the great marches on Washington, the campuses, the burnt-out ghettoes. Those were the stories I had been concerned with and so our paths had crossed. But we'd never really had a chance to sit down and talk about anything except the latest crisis. Always Tom was too much in the thick of things, hurrying along to the next demonstration, the next court case, the next confrontation. Now I order some coffee from room service and we begin to talk. Tom tells me he was born into a lower-middle-class Catholic family in Detroit, where his father was an accountant with Chrysler. His family had no connection with the labor movement. They lived in Royal Oak, a middle-class suburb of Detroit, and Tom went to Father Coughlin's parochial school. He never heard while he was growing up of Coughlin's career as a controversial radio priest, his challenge to the New Deal and of his being silenced by the Archbishop. That had been hush-hushed by his family. So was the fact that there were racial convenants in the deeds of all the houses in Royal Oak. From this conventional and protected background Tom had gone to the University of Michigan Journalism School and became editor of *The Michigan Daily*, the University paper. He hoped to be a foreign correspondent.

His mind, then, as far as I could understand, reflected a stereotype of middle-class thinking, probably not too unlike my own when I was going to the University of Minnesota and working on the school paper thirty years earlier.

Then a couple of rows broke out. This was 1960. A bunch of kids were expelled when they complained of being required to wear suits and ties in the lunch room and an argument arose over a white coed who had dated a black in a coffeehouse. Tom took up these causes in his paper. He didn't think of them as political issues and he thought that if the professors knew the facts they would right the injustices. But they didn't. They supported the deans and Tom was startled and shocked. Just about this time the young students in the South were beginning their lunch-counter sit-ins and this made him think more deeply. I told Tom his experience had been remarkably like my own as editor of the University of Minnesota Daily. I had crusaded on a trivial issue, the right of students to smoke in the library vestibule, and had been expelled for my pains. I had suffered shock and disillusion much like his, but there the parallel halted. I was expelled during the Depression days and the first thing I did was to go out and get a job. Tom followed a different path. He graduated in 1961 and went to the South, where the young people were rising up and acting on their political grievances. He went to Atlanta and plunged into work in the northern Mississippi voter-registration campaign.

It was out of these experiences, particularly his exposure to the student movement in the South, that Tom's politicization began. This led him to the Port Huron, Michigan, meeting in June, 1962, where Students for a Democratic Society was organized and in which Tom was to play a leading role for several years.

In the summer of 1963 he joined the big demonstration in Washington. He was becoming optimistic that Kennedy was moving in the right direction. The President had made a start toward enforcement of civil rights and in his American University speech he gave a signal to the Soviet Union for detente. Momentum was picking up. Then came the assassination. Tom can still feel his grief at the death of JFK. The moment for conciliation and consolidation was lost. Oswald's bullet smashed it all. Tom threw himself into the slum of Newark (most of his friends still focussed on the South, although the blacks were rapidly taking over the Southern movement), where he felt the worst of the problems were festering, and in this urban disaster area he began the painful process of trying to create an integrated action movement.

In those days Tom was almost hostile to the idea of the peace movement. He saw the fight against the war as not much more than an escape from the terrible problems at home, the ones which surrounded him in Newark, but by the summer of 1965 he was himself drawn into antiwar activities. So when Apteker and Lynd wanted a young radical to go with them to Vietnam he was delighted. Just the same he came back to the Newark ghetto after his return from Hanoi. I remembered that. I remembered he had given me the telephone number of a lawyer in Newark when I saw him that day in 1965. The lawyer, he said, would always know how to get in touch with him.

The coffee had arrived and sat on the table getting cold as Tom talked on. He was on to the Chicago convention of 1968 now, the dividing line for so many of Tom's generation, the chaos that had led to the famous trial of the Chicago Seven, of whom Hayden, of course, was one.

He has still, he said, not sorted out in his mind all the events at the Chicago Democratic Convention. Was it really an uncontrolled police riot? Did the officers simply go off on a rampage of their own? If not—who was behind it and what was their objective? There had, of course, been wild rumors long before the riot, long before the convention began, in fact, that violence was certain to break out. I had gone to Chicago weeks in advance and reconnoitered the scene, making plans for having *Times* reporters at the spots where trouble was likely and setting up special communications links for them.

Hayden had the feeling that planned provocation of violence might have fitted someone's objective. There had been reports that the leaders of the demonstrations, himself included, would be indicted *before* the convention opened. Who could have wanted that? Chicago was, after all, what Hayden regarded as a critical moment in history—the moment at which the dream of the American Century was fated to collide with the impossibility of its fulfillment. The government structure had been badly distorted, the nation was mired deep in an unpopular war. Something had to give.

What Hayden seemed to be hinting was that a kind of *götterdämmerung* may have been building up around Chicago, a mood of pulling everything down to the crash of police billies, the stench of tear gas and the whine of sirens around the Hilton Hotel. To me the scenario seemed too melodramatic and yet the times had been bizarre, there *were* unanswered questions. Nothing really could be ruled out.

During the trial of the Chicago Seven, Tom went on, there was serious talk around the defendents about the desirability of going underground. The Seven had been indicted in March of 1969 and the trial lasted from September, 1969, to February, 1970. There was lots of paranoia. The student movement had been broken. Some of the best and the brightest had turned to underground terror. Many thought that Nixon was about to bring to America a form of fascism (and many aspects of Watergate tended to make that suspicion plausible). The argument was made that the Chicago Seven should not sit quietly waiting the end of the trial. The verdict was certain to be guilty. They did not expect Judge Hoffman to allow them free on bail. The Court of Appeals would support him and there would be no release. They would stay in jail, serving their sentences of five to ten years and, in the course of their terms, they would be killed, either in the manner of Attica or by any other of a thousand "accidental" means.

Tom took the opposite side. He insisted that they must fight for the conscience of the jury and go on to the appeals court to win and bring public opinion over to their side. Tom confessed that at times it seemed as though anything was possible, particularly when the Panthers, Fred Hampton and Mark Clark, were shot down in their Chicago apartment under a police fusilade.

But, Hayden said, all of these events turned the public around. Respectable and responsible Americans began to feel that things had gone far enough. The reaction set in. The moratorium demonstration in the fall of 1969 was very big. In the end the Seven had followed the traditional route. They had been convicted, released on bail, appealed, won retrial and finally been acquitted in the autumn of 1973.

Yet, in back of it all, Hayden persisted, the Administration could have been trying to play out a scenario: first, arrest the radicals; then, attack the liberals; then, the press; then, the straightjacket for the whole of society.

I could understand that such a theory might arise in the tension of the Chicago events, but looking back on the tangle of personalities and policies which came together in the Nixon White House it seemed a bit too pat. Nothing the Nixon people did in their maze of clandestine operations ever really hung together. Even if the night porter had not noticed the taped door, the events called Watergate were bound to blow, sooner or later. Too many people knew, too many were bungling, too many were at swords' points.

When the trial finally ended, it put a period to an era in Tom's life. The movement to which he had devoted himself was smashed. It now suffered every kind of problem—sectarianism, self-destructiveness, irrational violence. The younger movement leaders blamed the older ones; no one seemed to talk the same language anymore; the women attacked the men as chauvinists; the Panthers attacked the whites; the whites resented the blacks. There was every sign that the show was over. Tom did not go back to Newark after the trial. He came to the Coast, where he had lived for a while as a child. He settled in the Bay area and got into the alternative culture movement. He was active for a while in the People's Park confrontation and tried to work with the Panthers in Oakland. Then, in 1971 he began to teach at Immaculate Heart College and at Pfizer College in Claremont. He showed slides and films to his students and played music about Vietnam. It was something new for him and it seemed to put his knowledge of Indochina to a useful purpose. Around this time he met Jane Fonda and they began to develop the Indochina Peace Campaign, which by 1972 had become a national movement with chapters all over the country. He and Jane got married, went a couple of times to North Vietnam and he wrote another book. By 1973 and 1974 he was doing some lobbying in Washington on Vietnam and teaching classes for members of Congressmen's staffs, through the courtesy of Congressman Dellums's office.

By this time his activities had gained more legitimacy because of Watergate and he himself was moving into a new political role, the role which had led to his decision to challenge Tunney.

"By the way," Tom said, "Would you like to go out with me tonight? We have a couple of meetings."

I quickly agreed. I had been hoping he would propose this. I badly wanted to see what the scene was like on California's new political front.

We went down and got into a yellow Volvo station wagon. "Actually," Tom said, "this is my wife's car. I drive an Impala."

As we drove he continued to talk about what had brought him into the Senate race. He had felt there were two ways he could go when the war came to an end—into journalism, which was where he had originally been headed at Michigan in 1960, or into politics. He couldn't immediately make up his mind. Both were important areas. Journalism seemed particularly attractive after Watergate and the flood of new investigatory reporting. As the war sputtered toward its ending, he talked with people in Washington about the future. He had gotten to know a good many former McGovern people. They agreed that what the country needed after Vietnam and Watergate was something which reflected the lessons of both, something that would go beyond the New Deal, something that would capture national attention and begin to vitalize the nation after its long trauma.

One way of getting started which occurred to Tom was to run as a delegate to the Democratic National Convention. He mentioned this to a friend who said what he really ought to do was run against Tunney for the Senate nomination and lose and then run again. This was in January of 1975 and Tom didn't think the idea was too realistic. But the more he explored it the more he began to wonder. He had worked in Berkeley in the 1971 elections, but his first real exposure to major politics came in 1974 when he covered Jerry Brown's campaign for governor for *Rolling Stone*. He learned how a state-wide campaign was set up, the mechanics of reaching the voters, the detail of building a campaign organization. He saw Jerry Brown as a post-Watergate phenomenon and spent a lot of time analyzing the crowds he drew, the way reporters covered candidates and the way Brown responded to the issues.

The more he thought about it the more attractive the Senate idea seemed. He explored the issues and began seriously to figure out whether he should undertake the race and if he did what form his campaign should take. By May he had made up his mind to run and he announced his intention in June.

By this time we were turning into a narrow street, just off Neilson, a block or so from the Santa Monica beach, a street of California bungalows of the 1930s, packed as tightly together on forty-foot lots as the developers could pack them, houses jammed so close they stood in perpetual darkness. Tom swung his car up a driveway beside a small white bungalow where children were playing with yellow and red plastic toys. Standing on the sidewalk in front of the house were Dick Flacks, chairman of the Santa Barbara University Sociology Department who is a specialist on the SDS, and his wife and Fred Branfman, who is Hayden's "policy coordinator."

Tom went in to change his clothes and Branfman and I stood on the sidewalk and talked for a while. His job was to research the issues and develop possible positions for Tom. Fred had been working with Tom on Vietnam since late in 1973. He was impressed with the way Tom thinks, the strategic quality of his thinking, his careful analysis of how to get from one point to another. He knew no one else on the Left who had this quality and admitted that it was a source of some estrangement on the part of the Left. But, Fred thought, Tom's thinking was very similar to that of the Vietnamese. They believed that there was a steady movement of history, leading in each stage to a higher plane than had been reached before. That, he said, was the way Tom thought.

The campaign was particularly interesting to him, Fred said, because it was the first time in years he had thought of anything but Vietnam.

I asked Fred, whom I had known slightly for some years, how he had gotten into the Vietnam movement. Branfman said he had grown up in Great Neck, where his father moved after a struggle upward from hard times in Brooklyn. Fred went to the University of Chicago and then Harvard and when the war and the draft came on he went to Tanzania and worked there, teaching English at first and then agriculture. He had actually wanted to join SNCC, but his father had gotten upset so he went to Tanzania instead and later to Laos. Seeing the war in Laos was what really radicalized him.

We went into the bungalow. Tom had vanished. Jane appeared in slacks, looking like any harassed young mother, and Fred and I sat talking in a bare living room, a red shag rug covering the floor and a basket of dried flowers in the fireplace. The house looked more camped in than lived in. Tom's campaign manager, Ed Zimmerman, lived in the house next door. Fred lived across the street and campaign headquarters was around the corner. It was kind of a Hayden compound.

Finally Tom emerges. He had put on a blue jacket and wears gray trousers and a gray silk tie. His hair, I notice, is longish but not *that* long. We get into the Impala. Ed Zimmerman, the campaign manager, is driving and I sit beside him. Tom sits in the rear and hunches forward to talk to me. They have had five hundred meetings so far of the kind we are going to tonight. They have thirty or forty of them a week. These are fund-raising and organizational meetings. They've raised about one hundred thousand dollars so far but the campaign costs about one thousand dollars a day. What Tom is doing is laying down his fundamental organization, the framework for the future, for the actual campaign and beyond the campaign. He is working inside the Democratic Party and with the labor unions to build his organization. A young man who is handling publicity remarks that the outlay every week just for clothing for campaign workers is considerable. He hasn't worn a jacket or a tie in his whole life. Now he wears them all the time. Someone has told him there is a new way to tie ties, the bigger ones they wear these days. Now he will have to learn how to tie his tie and get used to these new clothes.

The theme which he is using, Tom says, is that the radicalism of the Sixties is the realism of the Seventies. He feels the country has come to the end of the age of expansion and has entered a decline in terms of real growth. His ideas are designed to meet these new needs.

The first meeting is in Santa Ana, not far from Disneyland. We pass a great skyscraper lighted up and from its roof blazes a big lighted cross. We turned off the freeway and have some trouble finding the apartment block where the meeting is being held in its "community room." When we come in we duck under red-white-and-blue banners and a big sign proclaims: THE SPIRIT OF '76 IN '76—TOM HAYDEN FOR SENATOR. NOW IS THE TIME TO COME TO THE AID OF YOUR COUNTRY. There are Tom Hayden tee shirts and a homemade buffet of potato salad, coleslaw, hot chafing dishes, cold cuts, beans, chili, celery stuffed with cheese, carrot sticks, cheese, crackers and olives laid out with red-white-and-blue paper napkins. Tom seems a little surprised. "This is all their doing," he says, "the local people. Their layout, their slogans, everything."

There are sixty or seventy people here, perhaps more, mostly young but a sprinkling of middle-aged and some older ones. The prime mover in this group appears to be Ed Miller, a retired Marine colonel who spent five and a half years in prison in Hanoi. He is a strong handsome man with long brown hair, a bush jacket, a black moustache and a friendly manner. He is in his early forties and is going to law school. He would make an attractive candidate himself. Tom grabs something to eat while talking to the people who surround him. This will be all he eats this evening. He didn't have time for a bite at home.

Miller stands on the staircase and introduces Tom. He says he met Tom a year ago: "He brought the Vietnam war to an end. I present the next people's senator from California."

Tom speaks casually. He is actually preaching a kind of

people's socialism but there are no words to frighten his middle-class audience. His approach is all common sense and plain talk. There is no simple answer to our economic problems. Hard times will continue. Our incomes are lower than 1964. We've reached our limit in historic expansionism and manifest destiny. We're reaching the limits of structural imperialism. The middle class has to foot the bill. We must have an economic bill of rights. A decent job at a decent wage should be constitutional obligation. Fifteen percent of next June's college graduates will

Tom Hayden and Jane Fonda, his wife. Tom symbolized the protests of the 1960s, culminating in the Chicago trial. Now he's into mainstream politics. (Courtesy, ASSOCIATED PRESS)

be unemployed. We can't have this kind of unemployment for the rest of the century. We must have full employment, health-security legislation, the right to a job, health care and hospitalization. This must be free. We must cut medical costs sharply.

"Dreamland is gone," Tom says, "Disneyland is just disneyland."

I'm interested in this line. Lots of people in this area work at Disneyland and I've been told that its business is not what it used to be, that in California terms it is beginning to get old and people are worrying about its future.

Tom makes circular movements of his hands as he talks. He never lifts his voice. It is all conversational and low key. He is talking in the living room with friends, not making a political speech. He talks about equalizing the tax burden, increasing taxes on corporations and particularly on multinationals that run off to Mexico and deprive Californians of jobs.

Is Orange County too conservative for Tom? The answer is No! This line gets applause and some chuckles. Orange County used to be the most conservative county in the country. Now it is rapidly changing with the spillover of lower- and middle-income families from Los Angeles.

The only frontier left, Tom says, is improving the quality of our own life in our own country.

Before we slip away—Tom is not much of a handshaker as politicians go—I meet Jim Klein, one of Tom's principal Orange County organizers. He is a husky man of six feet four, blond, broad shouldered. He is a Catholic and has seven children. He is an outdoors writer, a great hunter and opponent of gun control. He has written books on gold mining and is an opponent of abortion laws. He is also one hundred percent for Tom.

Our next stop is Newport. We are working a coastal strip that begins at Santa Monica and sweeps down as far south as Laguna Beach. This strip is largely populated by young people, income oriented, upwardly mobile, open-minded in politics. They are very different from the cartoon image of Orange County neanderthals and the huge colonies of Middle West expatriates, come to California to retire or to work in the benign climate.

The Newport meeting is held in a whitewashed one-story architects and designers office, which houses an art gallery. It is a more sophisticated milieu than the Santa Ana meeting. These are young mod people wearing saddle-stitched blue jeans, expensive sports clothes, white Ground Grippers, sandals, fashionable slacks and sports shirts. The men have contoured haircuts and the women wear their hair loose and blond. They have glasses of scotch and soda in their hands and they pay no attention to the art which is going to be auctioned off for Tom's benefit. There is a girl who will draw you a caricature or a pastel in seven minutes for three dollars, a flautist and a guitarist. All very Southern California chic.

Tom gets on a table and starts talking. He uses a slightly different line with these people. If Nixon, Agnew and Mitchell had had their way he'd be in jail today. Now they are in jail and he is running for office.

Someone asks whether his past image as a radical is going to hurt his campaign. His response: What past image? There are cheers and laughs. If you weren't called something bad during Watergate and the war, says Tom, then you weren't there. He hits at the CIA, at multinational corporations, at the assassinations. The bubble has burst, he says, the dream is shattered. People had believed we had a civilizing mission in the world— to spread democracy. That image is broken.

I think as Tom talks. This *is* a different world from New York. No one in his right mind would schedule a political fundraiser in Westchester or Fairfield counties on a Saturday night, and if he did no one would be present. But here are two hundred smart young people obviously enjoying themselves. And there was the coffee-klatsch crowd in Santa Ana as well. It tells you something about the available alternatives in Southern California.

"What we believed we were," Tom says, "we were not. What we thought we had—we had not."

A television crew from a local station is taking Tom's picture and sweeping the crowd of his listeners. Tom runs through the points of his platform much as he did earlier. He puts a bit more emphasis on environment and gets a big hand when he calls for the use of solar energy by sunny California. His strongest remarks are addressed at the multinationals and he calls for sharp defense cuts. He gets his biggest applause when he says that if it takes Ralph Nader as Secretary of Defense to cut the military budget—then so be it.

He winds up saying: What I want is your hope. Give us your hope and your belief. We have to have your spirit.

Henry Fonda, Tom's father-in-law, is introduced briefly, congratulates his daughter, Jane, in her good sense in marrying Tom and the evening is over. Tom is riding back to Los Angeles with Henry Fonda, so we say good-bye. He is going to San Francisco early Sunday morning to hold a press conference and release what he calls a very strong statement about the CIA. I ride back with some of Tom's associates. They are excited about the campaign. They think it is going well and they say that Tunney is beginning to show signs of some worry. They believe that they have a chance of beating Tunney. They agree that there are quite a few Movement people and former Movement people who are antagonistic to Tom and his campaign, but they think this comes from a conviction that any kind of working within the system is bad, per se. They point out that they all come out of the Movement themselves.

Zimmerman, Tom's campaign manager, is new to California. He comes from Chicago and likes the climate of California and the attitude of the people. He thinks they are easy to approach with new ideas because they had to detach themselves from Iowa or New York in the first place in order to come to the Coast. That was a big move. Now they have broken their old moorings and they are more ready to listen to new things.

For persons like themselves, who live and breath politics twenty-four hours a day, Zimmerman says, California is a place where you can make things happen. He loves the weather and doesn't miss the Chicago winters. He loves the beach. That has a special freshness and ease about it.

We get back to Los Angeles and drive up to the Beverly Hilton. One of the young men laughs. "It's kind of funny driving up here," he says. "I know this hotel so well. This is where Thieu always stayed when he came to the United States. Many a time I came here to picket him."

There was something about the Hayden campaign that bothered me and later on I talked about this with my son, Stephan, and his friend, Patricia. They live, temporarily they hope, in Venice just south of Hayden's enclave in Santa Monica. Venice is a kind of run-down artists' and writers' colony on the western ocean outskirts of Los Angeles. They came to California a year ago to live while Patricia gets her doctor's degree in history. They live the lives of exiles from the East Coast, observing California life but hostile to it.

It was interesting to talk with them about Hayden because both had been Movement people in the Sixties, part of the great explosion at Columbia. I could still see Stephan and a girl friend walking into a very big cocktail party on Eighty-fourth Street, both in revolutionary leather jackets, Stephan's hair wind-blown and touseled, the girl's straight as straw, just out on bond after being swept up in one of the police swoops that thrust half of Columbia's young people into jail, the smart New Yorkers clustering around them in awe, as if they had just come back from the storming of the Winter Palace. I could still hear the wild denunciations by the young Movement people of every facet of the society which they knew and their calm certainty that Revolution awaited on the morrow.

But now these young people had turned their faces sternly against the dream and the excitement. They had cut physical ties with Movement people long since. They had turned to their own inner preoccupations, poetry and history, and the prosaic but urgent tasks of making a living. Yet, they had not given up a deep skepticism about the system. California had not changed this.

What bothered me about Hayden, I told them, was the plastic quality of his campaign. He was as much against the war, big government, big corporations, the system and all the rest as ever. But his rhetoric was tailored to tranquilization. That seemed to me to be the California model. Reagan had come on strong for lower taxes and less government and wound up with the biggest taxes on record and an ever-growing government. Governor Brown presented almost the ultimate development of a faceless image. I was told by a young Mormon that Brown was far too radical. But Stephan and Patricia (and many others whom I met) thought he might well be a reactionary. What to make of a politican who is seen by half the electorate as a conservative and half as a radical? This is packaging technique supreme and it is this packaging technique which Hayden, I suspect, learned as a political reporter covering Brown. Brown, I think, learned it from Reagan.

The technique was admirably adapted to the rootless California psyche, to people who never are quite certain who they are, who cut their ties with the past when they loaded into the camper or the bus and hit the highways for the Coast and who glide along in the California atmosphere with no real points of reference.

"There aren't any *standards* here," Patricia says. She is a very good student, but on the Coast she ranks as superlative. Stephan is a good poet but here the local poets, he feels, think he is too advanced. They feel uncomfortable with him. The truth is that what is missing in California is quality of life. The oranges are enormous but lack taste. The peaches are rosy beyond belief but lack tang. The people are lovely but disconnected from reality. They live within their own cocoons. A young man at Fullerton College tells me he asks the students from Orange County about something big that has happened in the world, the United Nations condemnation of Israel, for example. They say: "Gee, man, I hadn't heard about that." They grow up in a combustion-engine environment. They tune out the news. Many don't bother to watch television. They live in their own world and that is what they like about California life. Their parents are well-to-do and they inhabit their cars almost twenty-four hours a day from the time they are fifteen or sixteen.

People come to California, I say, to get out of the world—whatever world it may be—their job, their family, their environment.

You know, the young man says, if I had heard about Squeaky and Polly and Sara Jane when I was growing up I would have thought the world was coming to an end. Now people just take it. They don't see anything unusual. We've lost a President and two candidates to assassins. It's become the American way of life.

Stephan is the first member of my line of the family that began in Chepachet and continued through Canandaigua, Oregon, Mazomanie and Minneapolis to reach the West Coast. But it will be, it is clear, a transient thing. The Coast, he feels, is not a real place in the American sense. It is a kind of psyche floating on the edge of the old frontier. And I confess, I find nothing here that Hiram would have recognized except, perhaps, some of the young people who have turned to hammers and saws, paints and brushes, picks and axes. It is not the main stream but, even so, it may bring us some refreshment of spirit.

Of the future I shall venture no definite prophecies. It would be
a brave man who would venture them in any case.
　　　　　—*W. J. Cash*, THE MIND OF THE SOUTH, *1941*

WE WERE TWELVE at dinner, seated at a long table in the
living room of Dr. Mary Mebane's home on Senate
Street in Columbia, South Carolina. There was a cen-
terpiece of red and white carnations, silver on the white table-
cloth, paintings on the beige walls and a dramatic impression of a
Watusi warrior in welded iron in one corner. Dr. Mebane is a
regal woman and in her floor-length flowered gown I thought
she looked like an African queen.

I had not known Mary Mebane when I went to the
Carolinas in the uncertain winter of 1960. Something new and
not understood was happening. Young blacks, usually from
poverty-pinched black colleges, were slipping into Woolworths
and Kress, sitting down at the counters, and respectfully asking
to be served. In response the police arrested the young men and
women, hauled them off to jails, and the lunch counters closed
their doors. Better to serve no one than to serve a black.

In February, 1960, I came South to investigate this rather
puzzling phenomenon. It was to be my first extended reporting
trip into the South. Except for a time spent in Louisiana after
Huey Long's assassination in the late Thirties I had seldom
reported from the South. But from my travels through the back
country of Louisiana, the bayous and the red hill country of

northern Louisiana, I retained indelible images of the harsh poverty of the sharecroppers, of the regions where even the building of a road or a bridge suddenly moved a dark parish from the early nineteenth into the early twentieth century.

But if I had some understanding of the stark contradictions which still held much of the rural South in their grasp, this was the first time I would get a glimpse of racial and social problems in an urban setting.

I went first to North Carolina (the first sit-in had occurred at Greensboro in January). A constitutional test of the right of the students and other blacks to demand service at lunch counters and public places of business was starting its long course

Dr. Mary Mebane, associate professor of English, University of South Carolina. A writer and novelist, she is a regal woman who has endured. (Courtesy, IAN PATRICK)

through the courts. I attended a hearing in Raleigh and that evening went to dinner with some of those involved in the case. There were half a dozen of us, black and white, and the first problem was where to eat. We could not go to any hotel or downtown restaurant. Our mixed group would be instantly told to leave. In fact, we probably would be arrested like the young challengers of the sit-in movement. We finally went to a very clean, very plain restaurant in the "colored" district of Raleigh. It was almost empty. We sat in the back of the room and the black proprietor kept an eye out nervously. I was nervous, too. If it was not actually against the law in Raleigh for blacks and whites to eat together in a public place (even in the "colored" section), it was flatly against local custom. If a roving squad car came by, there could be serious trouble—this in "enlightened" North Carolina, proud of its leadership in establishing better race relations.

A day or two later I went to South Carolina, where more serious trouble was building up. In Orangeburg, South Carolina, there were what I called in my article for *The New York Times* "two Negro colleges," South Carolina State and Claflin College. A thousand or more college students marched into the center of Orangeburg, converging on Memorial Plaza. They sang hymns as they walked peacefully along the street, whites watching in curiosity and some apprehension. When the black students got to the center of town state police, sheriff's deputies and local police converged, firing tear gas and spraying them with fire hoses. The column broke apart under the attack. About three hundred and fifty students were rounded up by the police and, drenched and choking, herded into an improvised stockade in a parking lot beside the county courthouse. There they stood, neatly dressed, dignified, singing "God Bless America" and "The Star-Spangled Banner." Later they held a prayer meeting. They were charged with breach of the peace and released on a bond of ten dollars apiece. In Columbia nine students were arrested attempting to get service at a downtown lunch counter.

Governor (now Senator) Ernest F. Hollings warned of outside agitators and said the blacks should not think they could "violate any law, especially if they have a Bible in their hands. Our law-enforcement officers have their Bibles, too."

I talked with Hollings in his old-fashioned office in the domed State Capitol Building, the same building where South Carolina had ratified the resolution of secession in 1861. He was a handsome man with a reputation for political liberalism, especially in contrast to such classic South Carolina figures as Senator "Cotton Ed" Smith. He seemed to me to be genuinely puzzled at the sudden agitation sweeping the young black community. He had thought race relations were improving, particularly with the expansion of South Carolina's textile industry. He was worried that the unrest would kick back at his efforts to entice northern industry to South Carolina. Without the industry he did not see how the state could make the economic progress necessary to move forward with better education and better social programs for both black and white. In private he did not sound as hard-line as he did in public, a pattern I quickly became familiar with as I travelled in the South. In public the politician would "holler nigger" and "wave the bloody shirt." But in private he often expressed concern about an emerging social and political situation which he found difficult to comprehend. I learned, too, that private doubts and anguish did not stay the politician's hand when it came to the use of force.

In 1960 I met no blacks in a social setting anywhere in the South, and only on one or two occasions did I visit a black home for a formal interview. Each time it was nervy, almost conspiratorial. It reminded me of visits to Russian friends during Stalin's day, the furtive slipping out of the Metropol Hotel, the quick walk to the Metro (trying to make certain I had not been followed by one of the "boys" who lounged all day in the hotel lobby), the changes from train to train to throw off pursuit, the dash through the door of the flat (to avoid scrutiny by other members of its communal population), the whispered conversation, the relief at getting back to the hotel, hopefully having avoided surveillance.

Now I am sitting at Mary Mebane's dinner table in Columbia. The other guests around the table are all black. They are members of the black intelligentsia in South Carolina, many from the University of South Carolina, at Columbia, where Mary Mebane is associate professor of English, others from Orangeburg, some from state government, some professional people. Later on another eight or ten guests will join us, some black some white. It is an unusual evening for me but not for them. We are crossing no lines, setting no precedents. It may be the first time I have sat down to dinner in a black home in Carolina with black and white guests. But it is not a novelty to the Carolinians.

I am struck by the sturdy self-confidence of my new black

acquaintances and I think I know on what it is founded. I know Mary Mebane and I have some knowledge of what her life has been. The other lives differ in detail, but all have one common characteristic: they have *endured*.

Mary Mebane grew up in grinding poverty in the back country of Durham County, North Carolina. Her father was a farmer but he could not make enough to support his small family, Mary and her two brothers. He peddled his fruit and vegetables in the streets of Durham. Her mother worked her whole life in a tobacco factory. Her father died when she was a small child and Mary's going to school was a constant struggle. Somehow, she managed to get through high school and then, by working at every moment she could, put herself through North Carolina College at Durham, a black college, no integration while she was there, with a double major in English and music. She went out to teach in a succession of piney-woods Carolina black schools, then back to college, studying, working, saving, driving herself or being driven by some energy that had her in its grasp, getting her master's degree, getting her Ph.D at Chapel Hill and at last in 1965 settling down to teach at Orangeburg in South Carolina State College, technically an integrated school but still overwhelmingly black.

Her life was often demeaning and frightening. Especially traveling at night on the great busses over the Carolina roads, north or south, never knowing when some white brute might hurl an unspeakable epithet or commit an act of violence. Orangeburg seemed a haven. She had *arrived* at Orangeburg. The long, hard struggle was over. The first day she came to the university she saw a painting of a brown madonna and child by a black artist, Leo Twiges, hanging on a wall. "I had to have it," she remembers. Twiges let her pay for it, five dollars now, three dollars next month. It was, I suppose, a symbol of her new life and it hangs on Mary's living-room wall today, the first thing you see when you enter the door. The new life. The academic world. An end to the fear, the violence, the raw poverty.

So it seemed. On the evening of February 8, 1968, Mary went to bed in the front room of the rather large house in which she lived, just a block off campus. It had been an exhausting day, filled with tensions. An angry dispute had boiled up over the right of black students to use a bowling alley a couple of blocks away. No great issues seemed to be involved but the owner of the bowling alley permitted white students to use his premises and turned the blacks away and so it came to be a matter of principle. There had been some demonstrations and a good bit of pushing and shoving. The weather was bitter cold and police turned fire hoses on the black students. On this day the faculty had met all day trying to find a solution. The students had gathered in angry conclave. The state and city mustered police forces. When Mary went to bed the situation had still not been resolved. She lived just one street away from the campus. Next to her house there was a small building, which had been a barber shop, but now was being used for a voter-education project. Mary had sometimes worried that someone might try to burn the little building down. And this was in her mind when she was awakened by the noise of motors in the narrow street. She looked out the window and saw a line of cars in front of the house. She put on her wrapper and opened the door. The street was half filled with men, standing in the dusk. She was frightened. She did not recognize them. "What are you doing here?" she asked. No one replied. She stood uncertain a moment. She was about to say: "If you don't tell me I'm going to call the police." Then one man spoke in a broken voice: "They're shooting our students up there." The dim figures in the gloom were Mary's fellow faculty members at South Carolina State, taking refuge from the fusillade of police guns, which killed three students and wounded many more.

"I don't remember what happened after that very well," Mary says and even now her voice breaks and she puts a hand to her head. "First they said one was killed, then another. And there were the horror stories from the hospitals, how the students had to wait for treatment, the awful remarks."

Mary is still too upset to talk much about that night. She broke down the morning after the massacre and spent some days in the hospital herself. When she came home it was like coming to occupied territory. There were armored troop carriers everywhere. Military outposts around the campus. She wanted to take a picture but was afraid to use her camera.

"To find yourself the enemy in your own country," she remembers. "I was afraid to use my camera. I was afraid if they saw the flash they would shoot at me."

Most of the guests have gone. Only an artist, Arthur Rose, Sr., and Alice Gallman, a registered nurse and supervisor of a large unit in the South Carolina Department of Mental Health, remain.

Rose is the man who did the sculpture of the Watusi warrior. He goes out to his car and returns bearing a large collage. "I wanted you to see this," he says. He teaches art at Claflin College in Orangeburg.

Mr. Rose is a small man with quick gestures and he wears a large black-velvet bow tie, a ribbed white shirt and white patent-leather shoes.

His collage is rough and brutal, filled with figures of helmeted troopers, clippings from *The State*, Columbia's newspaper, about the massacre, and the eye is drawn to a grim wooden box labeled NIGGER BONES, held in the arms of a sheriff's deputy.

We look at the painting. One headline reports the refusal of the grand jury to indict the troopers.

"That's why," Mary says sadly, "I could never get excited about Kent State. The whole country was upset by Kent State. But Orangeburg happened three years earlier and who knows that it happened?"

Mrs. Gallman nods her head.

"That's why I still don't celebrate Christmas," she says. "I celebrate Thanksgiving but I don't go to the stores and buy anything for Christmas."

The black community organized a boycott of the white merchants of South Carolina after Orangeburg and Mrs. Gallman's refusal to go Christmas shopping stems from those days.

Mrs. Gallman is fifty-three. She is a friend of Mary's and came early to help with the dinner. She grew up in the Carolina Piedmont, one of nine children in a sharecropper family so poor that the children often went for a day or even two with nothing to eat. The plantation owner was so poor he could not afford to bulldoze roads to the huts where the black families lived beside a marsh, drawing their water from a common spring. Only two members of Mrs. Gallman's family survive, most died in infancy or childhood, four in one bitter year. She, herself, was married at fourteen, had the first of her six girls and two boys at sixteen. She has given college education to all but two of her children—two are still at the university.

She put herself through the university, holds a registered-nurse's certificate, is a specialist in coronary problems, psychiatry and obstetrics and may go on and get a medical degree, for which she has already fulfilled many of the requirements.

How was this possible, I ask in wonder.

Mrs. Gallman smiles. She is a fine-looking woman with an earnest manner.

"You know down here white people are always saying 'I had a black mammy,'" she smiles. "Well, I had a white mammy."

She went to work for her white mammy as a personal maid when she was about twenty. From the start her relationship was not an ordinary one. Instead of the usual blue uniform with white collar and cuffs she wore pastel uniforms.

"She loved me," Mrs. Gallman says, "And I loved her. It was as simple as that."

Of course, it wasn't simple at all. Nothing is simple south of the Mason-Dixon Line. The guests at Mary's party talk as do dinner guests anywhere about the problems of living, about their houses, their apartments, the cost of things, politics.

But there are undercurrents. I talk with Charles McMillan, who is in charge of minority student affairs at the university. There are eighteen hundred full-time black students in a body of about twenty-three thousand. Six hundred blacks were accepted for admission and three hundred entered in 1975. Blacks are not exactly encouraged to come to the university. There is little financial assistance for them and subtle and not so subtle discrimination. The textbooks are hardly modern in their treatment of black history. Less than one percent of the faculty is black and only five are full-time tenured professors.

Like the other black intelligentsia McMillan has come up the hard way from Barnwell County, living in a house where he could see the stars at night through the roof and never had to ask whether it was raining because the rain came right in. Now he has moved along in the world. He and his mother have bought a good deal of acreage around Barnwell.

Things have changed but he and the other blacks are concerned about a rise in police violence. Four black males have been shot and killed in the past six months in various parts of the state—Moncks Corner, Florence, Greenwood and Orangeburg. The incidents have occurred, police insist, when blacks have been halted for arrest or investigation. There is a feeling that a pattern lies behind these outbreaks. A black activist named Redfern II (born James Redfern II, he legally changed his name to drop the "James") and his organization, Right On Nation, has been moving toward a more militant position, stimulated by concern over the shootings. Redfern was a straight-A student at the University of South Carolina in the 1960s. Most of Mary's friends know Deuce, as they call him, admire his brilliance and believe that Deuce is feared by the white community because he speaks his mind so boldly.

What, I wonder, is the Right On Nation?

"Well," says McMillan, "I suppose it wants to prove to blacks that they are not an inferior people, that whatever the whites can do, we can do it better."

I ask McMillan who is the hero of the black students.

The question troubles him. They really don't have heroes today. This is not a time when there is much action on the campus. The students are interested in getting ahead. Issues don't arouse them. For some perhaps Dick Gregory is a hero. In the past it was King and Cleaver and Brown. Maybe now that Cleaver is back in the United States he will again come to the fore. Julian Bond is respected. So are Shirley Chisholm and Barbara Jordan.

Do the students have any white heroes, I ask.

McMillan says quizzically: "You've got to be kidding!"

Mrs. Gallman shakes her head. A whole lot has gone on, she says, that no one knows about. Take herself for example. For eighteen months she was harassed by police. And this wasn't back in the sixties. This was in the last two years. Night after night they would follow her oar, tailgating her. They would halt her on the backroads to check her papers. Sometimes two or three times in an evening.

It stemmed, she thought, from an election in which she had supported the incumbent white sheriff over a white patrolman who resigned to try for the sheriff's job. Finally the police arrested her on a charge of failure to dim her lights and hauled her in to the courthouse. They roughed her up and tore her clothing. She called them cowards.

"I never have the sense to be scared," she said.

When she got to the courthouse, she announced that she would not go up the steps until she had talked to the sheriff. She held her ground and the sheriff appeared to find out what was going on. She told him she wanted to call her lawyer. The police said: "She can call anyone she wants. She can call the Governor if she wants."

So she called the Governor and was turned loose. After that she decided it was too dangerous to drive the backroads at night and moved to Columbia.

Mary and Mr. Rose agreed she had been wise to move. If

she had been a black male, they thought, she probably would have been shot. Whether true or not it was clearly what they believed.

So now I thought I was beginning to understand. South Carolina was not the South Carolina I had seen fifteen years before. A black intelligentsia was emerging. Most of these people felt that economically they were better off in the South (and blacks from the North, in small numbers, were returning for the same reason). But the old fear was not far in the past and it could return. Every black in the room had endured it. They did not look to lose any of the gains they had made. But they did not exaggerate. There were more leagues to cover before they reached a common goal and it would not be an easy journey.

Mary drove me back to the Carolina Inn, a fine new skyscraper hotel just beyond the university. By choice she lives in a tattered black ghetto five minutes from the university. Her apartment is bright and comfortable, but four similar flats one hundred feet away were destroyed the week before in a tornado that dipped down over Columbia, wreaking damage to the flimsy habitations of the blacks. As we leave her apartment we hear the deep-throated bark of police dogs. Most of the neighbors have dogs for protection. It's a high-crime area. We bounce over bumpy pavement onto the brightly lighted streets around the hotel. "It's a nice hotel," Mary says. "We often come here Saturday nights. They have good music and entertainment." As I pick up my key at the desk four or five handsome young men and women pass me, laughing and talking. The men are tall and well groomed, the women look as though their clothes come from Saks or Bonwits. All are black.

From Red Mountain, where a cast-iron Vulcan looks down five hundred feet to the sprawling city, Birmingham seems veiled in the poisonous fumes of distant battle. . . . More than a few citizens, both white and Negro, harbor growing fear that the hour will strike when the smoke of civil strife will mingle with that of the hearths and forges. . . .
—*Special to* THE NEW YORK TIMES *from Birmingham, Alabama,*
April 8, 1960

So began my report on Birmingham in 1960, a report which outraged the leaders and the "big mules" as the red-clay politicians called them, a report which the city officials violently denounced and which formed the basis of a libel action filed against me for $1,500,000 (and a similar suit against *The New York Times*) and my indictment by the grand jury of Bessemer, Alabama, a suburb, on forty-two counts of criminal libel.

In my dispatch I quoted a Birmingham resident as saying: "Birmingham is going to blow one of these days."

I suppose that nothing in my forty years of reporting caused such an explosion of indignation, not even going to Hanoi in the heat of the Vietnam War. I told in my dispatch of the tapping of telephones, the interception of mail, the informers, the provocations, segregation so complete that the streets, the sewer system and the water supply were about all the facilities shared in common (but drinking fountains were segregated). I told how books that featured black rabbits and white rabbits were banned and said that those who violated the rules of segregation were liable to retaliation by bombs, clubs, guns, knives, mobs and thinly disguised intervention of the police and the state apparatus. I quoted Birmingham's Police Commissioner Eugene Connor, commonly known as Bull, as saying: "Damn the law—down here we make our own law."

I did not say in my dispatch what I really felt, that the atmosphere of fear in Birmingham was worse than in the most paranoid years of Stalin's Russia, even worse than when I had made a long journey into eastern Siberia, into the heart of the slave labor prisons and found myself dogged at every step, night and day, by a goon squad of a dozen or more of plainclothes secret police in an area four thousand miles distant from the nearest American embassy.

I had checked into the Tutwiler hotel, a shabby relic of one-time grandeur, and begun to telephone around town. I encountered the kind of reserve I had known in Russia. People were reluctant to speak on the telephone and some even refused to see me. One man told me: "Remember Birmingham is no place for irresponsible reporting. Be careful of what you say and who you mention. Lives are at stake."

I thought I had been careful. But I learned that I had not been. After my dispatch was published, the police obtained from the hotel a record of all the numbers I had called. Each person who had the misfortune to receive a call was summoned before a grand jury. Some were imprisoned for refusal to testify as to the nature of our conversations. I was sorry then I had not used the comparison of Birmingham and Moscow. I was sorrier that I had not had the common sense to use the simple conspiratorial technique of the Moscow reporter—to use public telephone booths rather than the hotel phone.

Even in the dismal days of 1960 I had met brave and strong individuals in Birmingham who had not been cowed by the forces of racial violence and who were willing to stand up to the crowd. They were not many. Some were black and some were white and I admired them enormously.

It was years before the great libel cases finally came to trial and when they did, the verdicts were against the lone city commissioner who still pressed his case—Bull Connor. Not only did we win the cases, but they served to broaden even further the protection of the press against the use by public officials of the libel apparatus to cast a veil of censorship.

What I had predicted had tragically happened. Martin Luther King had come into Birmingham, been arrested and wrote his famous *Letter from a Birmingham Jail.* Four small black girls had been killed by a bomb at the Sixteenth Street Baptist Church in 1963. Almost every nightmare which had been dreamed under the brooding presence of Vulcan had been played out in life. Among the tragedies of the contemporary South and contemporary America, none equaled that of Birmingham. I felt no satisfaction in having foreseen what would happen in Birmingham. The reality had been too dreadful.

I had been back to Birmingham once since fateful 1960—to spend a few days while the libel actions were argued in court, to sit each day beside Bull Connor, to watch the forces of Southern courtesy and political malarky work their wonders until each morning we were greeting each other and listening to Bull bid us adieu ("Take care now, y'all").

I knew change had come to Birmingham—but how much, how deep, how real?

I landed on a gusty day at the Birmingham airport, all new since I had been there, was picked up by Cecil Roberts, a charming dynamic woman whom I sometimes think has enough energy to level Red Mountain single-handed if she has a mind to it, and drove into a new city—a new city physically, a city no longer dominated by the gloomy Vulcan and the perpetual acid smoke clouds of the great Tennessee Iron and Coal Co., steel mills, a city of lifting skyscrapers and glass towers, a civic center with concert halls for the symphony, stages for the theater (the Moscow Circus was now playing; the Moscow Symphony had just been here) and at the foot of Vulcan, where once stretched a wilderness of decaying warehouses one of the biggest and finest

1960: "Birmingham is going to blow one of these days." 1975: Bessie Estell, member of the Birmingham City Council and Birmingham's Woman of the Year. (Courtesy, IAN PATRICK*)*

universities in the country, all built since 1960. To be sure this was physical change—the silvery mobile in the South Central Bell building and the great mural along one wall; the huge coliseum being built for ice hockey and basketball teams to come; the Twentieth Street Mall with its holly and fruit trees. But this did not explain the dance groups, symphonies, theater companies, art exhibitions and galleries. The Tutwiler Hotel was gone—but what of its era? Everywhere I saw red-white-blue shields proclaiming Birmingham ALL AMERICA CITY. Kelly Ingram Park, where the stench of tear gas lingered for months in the 1960s looked trim and neat, bright grass, artistic plantings. It was a memorial to the first man from Birmingham killed in World War I, a black. When I first saw Birmingham, blacks were not permitted to enter it.

I admitted to Cecil I didn't recognize the town.

She gave me an impish grin and whisked me up to the eighteenth floor of a skyscraper. Here she had assembled for me the new Birmingham power structure. I had, I admit, eyes for only one of its members, Bessie Estell, Birmingham's Woman of the Year, newly elected member of the city council, the first black woman to be named Woman of the Year, the first black woman to be elected to the city council, where she joined two other blacks in a group of nine. Mrs. Estell is a delicate woman and she wore a lovely gray silk knit dress. When she speaks it is with precision and care. She had been nominated Woman of the Year by the Young Men's Business Club of Birmingham and elected from a field that included nineteen whites and seventeen blacks.

Just twenty years before Cecil Roberts had been Birmingham's Woman of the Year. "I think I was a bit emotional," Mrs. Estell says, "when I heard that they had picked me. But I remember what I said. I said: 'Birmingham has come a long way.'"

For years Mrs. Estell taught school in Birmingham, in, of course, a segregated black school. She was the school principal in a segregated black school in the terrible years of the early 1960s. The bombing at the Sixteenth Street Church, she felt, was like Pearl Harbor. After that the city seemed to come to its senses. The children in her school had been terribly disturbed by the violence. It took time for the trauma to subside. One thing was still on her conscience. No one had ever been apprehended for the deaths of the four little girls, yet she and others believed the identity of the perpetrators had been known.

During the past summer she had been in charge of arrangements for the largest convention Birmingham had ever had, sixteen thousand members of the Baptist Sunday School and Training Conference. It had filled every hotel and motel for one hundred miles around Birmingham. It had come off perfectly. Not a single incident of racial feeling.

And yet . . .

"We still have not arrived," she said firmly. "There is a lot we must do before we sleep."

Especially, she felt, in education. It must be improved, particularly in the countryside. And the crime rate must be brought down. This she saw as largely an economic problem.

Blacks are moving forward politically in Birmingham and in Alabama. She cited the career of Chris McNair, a Birmingham photographer who has done much work for large Birmingham corporations. He is a member of the state legislature and several white guests at the luncheon called him one of the outstanding Birmingham political personalities. He has been chosen chairman of the Jefferson County legislative delegation, which is predominently white. And, as all pointed out, his little girl was one of those killed in the bombing.

The bankers and industrialists agreed that Birmingham had put racial phobia behind it and that this had been accomplished by hard work on both sides, particularly by a Community Affairs Committee, black and white, which meets week-in, week-out every Monday morning at 7:30 to thrash out problems involving race.

The power structure had changed almost entirely. These were mostly young men in their late thirties and forties. Many had been recruited south to head large institutions or had moved to Birmingham from other parts of the South. They had no use for the racism of the Bull Connor era. That had given Birmingham the blackest name in the country. If nothing else it was bad for business. They were changing the town. No longer was it a blue-collar steel town. New industry was coming in, corporate headquarters and technological specialities, and then there was the university.

The university had given a new specific gravity to Birmingham's urban mass. It was the largest employer in town with 7,000 on its payroll and a budget of $130,000,000. It wielded a

Cecil Roberts of Birmingham, Alabama: a woman of hope and courage. She defied race hate and helped turn her city into a beacon of hope. (Courtesy, IAN PATRICK)

bigger wallop than TCI, the U.S. Steel subsidiary, whose payroll numbered 12,000. It brought thousands of students, black and white, to the city. Its faculty was young and open minded. Blacks moved up the middle-class ladder in the banks and insurance companies and as John Woods, who came down a few years ago from New York to head the First National Bank, said bluntly:

"Birmingham's consciousness has changed."

County Commissioner Ben Erdreich said: "There's no Bull Connor anymore and if there was one around he wouldn't last long."

(Bull had died three or four years ago after several years of partial paralysis and wheelchair existence.)

John Munro left the Harvard Divinity School in 1967 to join Miles College in Birmingham. He is a tweedy man and he has helped turn what I had seen in 1960 as a woebegone black college into a vital institution with 1,200 to 1,300 students, a $4,000,000 budget, a new law school and emerging role in the community. Most of the faculty and almost all the students are black. Once its largest field had been teacher training. Now it is business and it has become a recruiting ground for large corporations. Munro thinks that ultimately Birmingham may be predominantly a university town and not a heavy industry town. Cecil Roberts thinks the same. The students at Miles now seem interested in careers, not causes. What they want is quality instruction. Where are they going in life? To work. More and more to graduate schools. There is little left of the black militant movement, but there is a rising interest in prisons and the condition of black prisoners. Race may seem a dead issue in elections now but Munro is not certain it has gone for good. Blacks are sensitive to the conduct of the police and they are convinced that police discrimination against blacks must end.

Munro believes Birmingham desperately wants to be regarded as the ALL AMERICAN CITY. The image is tremendously important after the bad days of the 1960s. No one wants to tarnish the image and the town is still running scared.

Cecil mentions the new dignity of the blacks and her feeling that they now hold a better position in society than up north.

Munro agrees and adds. "Twenty-five years from now the issues of today may seem so strange as to be unbelievable."

When I tour the new university my conviction grows that Birmingham has shed its skin. This university has 14,000 students of whom 2,500 are black. Between eight and ten percent of the faculty are black. It has a $62,000,000 construction program underway and one of the finest medical facilities in the country has been developed. All but a small medical core of this has gone up since I first saw Birmingham in 1960.

In the evening we are again twelve for dinner. This time it is not at a ghetto apartment but the Mountain Brook Club across Red Mountain, beyond Vulcan, outside the city limits of Birmingham.

I put a question to the guests. Are they optimistic or pessimistic about the future—the future not only of Birmingham but also of our society and country.

Emery Cunningham speaks first. He heads a fast-growing publishing company which has been built on the base of the old farm publication, *Progressive Farmer* (1,100,000 circulation). He publishes *Southern Living* (1,250,000 circulation) and a growing list of very profitable books. His friends say he made a million dollars on one called *Jericho* last year.

He is very optimistic about the future of the United States, but he's worried about whether Birmingham can maintain its individuality and the South its special characteristics. He has great confidence in the young.

Mrs. David Roberts IV, a Northerner and wife of Cecil Roberts's son, feels negative. Money seems to have replaced ideals and there no longer are knights in shining armor. But she has a child of four. "I must be optimistic," she says with a wry smile.

Duard Le Grand is editor of the Birmingham *Post-Herald*, a Scripps-Howard newspaper. He was the first person I telephoned when I came to Birmingham in 1960.

He is very pessimistic. Maybe in one hundred years some good things will come to pass. But now he doesn't feel we are facing up to the basic race issue. It lies in the core city, but the whites have gone to the suburbs. No one at the dinner table lives in Birmingham city and the suburbs don't sympathize with the core and its black problems. He is afraid race conflict can wipe out all the progress.

Blacks continue to be shot in and out of jail. If the Supreme Court permits they will again go to the electric chair.

David Roberts IV teaches ethics at the university. He is pessimistic, too. The concept of physical existence of the seventeenth century has reached a peak. Society has found its highest aim in the protection of physical property. An artificial technology makes man a machine. People who could do something about this, the academics for instance, have not.

Mrs. S. Richard Hill, Jr., the wife of Dr. Hill, vice-president for university health affairs has a short answer: "I am an optimist."

David Roberts, Cecil's husband, calls himself "a pessimist." The younger generation may make some progress, but we are going to have to face the facts of all this deficit financing. He thinks the younger generation is better at facing facts than his own.

Mrs. Marvin Engels, wife of one of Birmingham's big real-estate developers, is bitter. She is the mother of two young people who have been turned from idealism to cynicism by seeing the cynical conduct of the older generation. She sees in our society no real leaders.

Bart Britz, head of a big steel-fabricating company, is both optimistic and pessimistic. He realizes that we have an obligation to help those out of work and he knows we have the ability to be the best in the world. But we have people who want our air one hundred percent clean. They aren't satisfied with ninety-eight percent, but the cost of those last percentage points is very great. Someone has to decide whether we want those last few points and how we are going to pay for them. There is no free lunch.

Dr. Hill is highly optimistic. He has been in Birmingham twenty years and when he sees the whole city turn around it is something to behold. He's optimistic in what's happening in medical science. When you see what can be done with the heart of a child to give it a normal life span, it makes you a natural optimist. But he worries about the work ethic of people.

Mrs. Le Grand is pessimistic. She thinks we've learned nothing and what we've learned we have forgotten. We have no leader who can tell right from wrong or say: this is the law. She believes we can pay for and give a lot more for clean air. She thinks we can walk a lot more, cut the heat down (she and her husband were the only people on the street who cut it down to sixty-six) and she'd like to stop those sons of guns who are speeding on the highways and using up her gas.

Mr. Engel calls himself a pessimist-optimist, a pessimist in the short run—the next fifteen or twenty years. It's the first time in ten or twelve years when his company hasn't even thought about building another shopping center. Of one hundred large shopping-center developers there is only one who has a project about to start. He lacks the confidence to predict three years ahead. But when he looks at the young people, then he thinks maybe things are beginning to turn around.

"What about Watergate?" Mrs. Le Grand asks. "That was supposed to turn us all around."

"Morals and honesty," Mr. Engel replies, "begin at home in the family and if we are moral at home then it will spill over into the government. I am impressed by the young people I saw working in the hotels up in New England last summer. I take heart for this country. We are big enough to grab ourselves by the bootstraps and get back on the right track."

"Life gets better every year," says Mrs. Hill.

Mrs. Britz thinks it all goes back to the individual and whether he is willing to give a better day's work and is an honest person.

"Doesn't everybody you know live better than they used to?" Cunningham asks.

Le Grand and David dispute Cunningham. They don't think the question is entirely a material one. Moreover, they are not so certain that blacks and everyday workers necessarily live better.

Cecil Roberts asked to speak last. She has a saying: put it down on paper. If she puts it down on paper she would call herself a pessimist. She thinks TV is the opiate of the people. They lose themselves in a fantasy world. But more books are being sold. And more newspapers. On the other hand, conversation and correspondence are lost arts. There is a lack of communication, person to person. Many people are more interested in things than in people. But she puts her money on people. She sees it in Birmingham. There is potentially some marvelous talent in the South. What happened in Birmingham happened because a few people cared. It's just amazing how out of the goodness of their hearts and from the bottom of their pocketbooks people have done things.

"I put down on paper," she says, "that I'm a pessimist, but looking into the crystal ball I'm an optimist."

David IV says what concerns him is distribution. Suppose you have one thousand units of happiness and a society that is half free, half slave and the units go entirely to the free. Is that society as happy as one where there are five hundred units of happiness and everyone gets one unit?

Cunningham recalls that when he was growing up in Alabama it was a country of malaria, mosquitoes, pellagra,

Saturday night murders, smallpox, infantile paralysis, political maneuvering. It wasn't until after World War II that it began to get rural electrification.

"What about starving people?" asks David IV.

Cunningham replies that there were more cultural things this fall in Birmingham than in the whole of Alabama in a year in those days. The poor people in Alabama live better than the rich people a few years ago.

David IV reiterates that the problem is just distribution of goods and the moral nature of the way goods are produced.

Le Grand says tartly: Per capita income fell in Alabama this year but I'm delighted to hear our bank holding companies are doing so well.

What worries Britz is capital formation. If we are going to progress in the higher arts and a better way of life we have to have a base. He is very much impressed with the Japanese. Their government stands behind business. They love their country. The Japanese really love their country.

Le Grand is outraged: You mean the Japanese love their country more than we love ours? I find that very hard to believe. That is the same system that produced Tojo.

Britz replies that the Japanese are a very honorable people. They are more honorable than some people in Europe whom we deal with.

Finally, the guests turn to me. What do I think? Am I a pessimist or an optimist?

I can't help laughing. For an hour these people who have turned a dark and dismal city into a bright almost joyous environment have been trying to convince me that if disaster does not stand at our door it is not very far distant. It is as charming a comedy as I have witnessed in many years. I tell them that. Some pessimists! If they could be turned loose on the country at large these pessimists would have it moving in a fashion that would make heads spin.

Oh, I know that there would be plenty of problems, but who seeing this small miracle could doubt the possibility of a greater one.

I talk for a long time with Cecil and David before we break up, for they are two people who have given their whole lives toward transforming an ugly dangerous community into a city of hope. I am certain they knew fear in the worst days when the telephone brought obscene threats, the mail was intercepted, and there was real danger of bombs or revolver shots.

But they faced up to that. Cecil was born in England, came to the United States as a youngster, grew up on Long Island and in New York. Her nature is not to be downed, and her husband, a naval officer in World War II and a member of an old and well-to-do Birmingham family, would never wobble in the face of peril.

Even in the worst times Cecil maintained bantering relations with Bull Connor and he assured her that the police followed her for her own protection and, as she admits, perhaps that was right. "Ol' Bull could have arrested me many a time," she says, "for doing decent human things like taking blacks to places where it was against the law. Of course he knew what I was doing, but he never arrested me."

Cecil has been involved in almost every kind of good works there is in Birmingham. She was a member of Governor Wallace's State Council on Arts and Humanities until recently.

"When I'm in Birmingham," she says, "I'm always telling people what I think is bad or what I think is wrong. And they believe I am a radical. But when I go outside Birmingham I am always telling people what a wonderful place it is."

Well, I think, Birmingham is not heaven. On the way to the airport I drive through dismal streets of shanty houses. It's not a heaven for blacks or whites and I don't for a minute think race feeling has vanished. But I've had a look at the city again from the ramparts of The Club, the exclusive pinnacle that stands on Red Mountain just beside Vulcan. By night Birmingham is not ugly. With its jutting new skyscrapers and the four hundred-acre campus at the foot of the mountain, it glitters like a field of Alabama stars. I agree with the cool words of Bessie Estell. Birmingham has come a long way and I do not think Wallace or anyone else will put it back into the swamp again. I riffle through some of the Chamber of Commerce literature. They are talking about the past and my eye is caught by a phrase: "A New York writer said of Birmingham in 1960: 'Every inch of middle ground has been fragmented by the emotional dynamite of racism.' " Well, they don't use my name. I recognize my words and must admit I never thought to see the day when my $1,500,000 "libel" would be drawn upon by Birmingham to tell the story of how it was.

So I come back again to my conviction of how complex is the story of the South, how easy it is to make quick and mistaken judgments in this land in whose pessimism we may find our own optimism. I remember the knot of fear that cramped my stomach the first time I walked the streets of Birmingham, a fear that was shared by those with whom I talked, black and white. That fear is gone and I do not think it can be found today in Vulcan's city.

It seems to me that the image of my country, once so fragmented, is beginning to come together. It is taking form not as a starry dream but a kind of cold-eyed reality, the reality which comes to people who have been through a lot, learned that they can take it, learned that they can get up from the floor and go another round, confident of ultimate victory, if not in this generation, then surely in the next. And the feeling, curiously, seems to me more certain among the Southern blacks and whites than among their Northern cousins.

There is, I think, more than a little of the spirit I identify with old Hiram transmitted down the country's bloodlines and the evidence is there for those who look for it.

I think now I will go back to New England where it all began, there to seek a final word from two of the wisest people I know, Judge Lawrence Brooks and his wife, Sue.

Judge and Mrs. Lawrence Brooks, keepers of the faith in the Citty Upon a Hill, builders of America, believers in America. (Courtesy, IAN PATRICK)

Wee shall be as a Citty upon a Hill, the eies of all people are upon us; soe that if wee shall deal falsely with our god in this worke wee have undertaken and soe cause him to withdrawe his present help from us, wee shall be made a story and a by-word through the world.

—*John Winthrop, 1630*

MORRIS LONGSTREET HALLOWELL was a Philadelphia merchant and a violent opponent of slavery. Most of his customers were Southerners and they threatened him with a boycott. He put a sign on the wall: I DO NOT SELL MY PRINCIPLES WITH MY GOODS. It ruined his business but he held his head high. One day he called on his good friend Lincoln in the White House. The President was busily writing. He looked up and said: "Hallowell, is there a 'p' in empty?"

Hallowell's son fought in the Civil War. He and his friend Oliver Wendell Holmes were wounded at Antietem, Holmes through the neck, Hallowell in the arm. When the surgeon finished with Holmes he turned to Hallowell. "If I had a piece of flat wood," he said, "I think I could save that arm." Holmes glanced around the farmhouse and saw a banjo clock. He ripped off its back and the surgeon fashioned a splint which saved Hallowell's arm.

Young Hallowell, wounded at Antietem, was the father of Sue Hallowell Brooks. She and her husband, Judge Lawrence G. Brooks, are my oldest friends—not in years of our friendship but in years of their age. The Judge was ninety-five on February

21, 1976; Sue was ninety-three on December 19, 1975. They stand together like a monument to the Mayflower compact.

The last time I visited them in their house at Pleasant Bay on Cape Cod, we took a dip at seven in the morning, walking together down a steep trail that leads from the sand cliff, where their house has stood since 1888. Later Judge Brooks went for a row as he has almost every summer day of his more than nine decades of life and the next day he went sailing in the little boat which has been his favorite for the last fifty years.

The fathers of these remarkable people (the Judge is New England through and through; Sue's Quaker parents were transplanted to Boston from Philadelphia after the Civil War) were *contemporaries* of Hiram, born ten or fifteen years before Hiram's death. The Brookses' lives span half the existence of the Republic.

From the Brookses flows a sense of continuity of American life which is almost impossible to describe. Judge Brooks was seven years old when the Pleasant Bay house was built. Its weathered shingles and plain wooden interior have hardly changed. Nor have his principles and those of Sue altered from the plain doctrines of truth, honesty and justice of their forebearers.

But there is nothing antique about the minds of Lawrence and Sue Brooks. There is not an issue of the day which they do not follow with intense interest. There were no stronger opponents of the Vietnam war than the Judge and his wife and the first article the Judge wrote for the Op-Ed page of the *Times* called upon J. Edgar Hoover to retire because of his advanced age (seventy-one). The Judge had just quit his post on the Medford Court at the age of eighty-nine. The Judge has been a participant in Republican politics since he was graduated from Harvard in 1902. Theodore Roosevelt was his hero. He thought T.R. was the "McGovern of his day" but he broke with him in 1916 when T.R. tried to transfer his following to the camp of Henry Cabot Lodge. Judge Brooks thinks T.R. was the superior of F.D.R., "that tricky man," but confesses that T.R. was too vain and this kept him from greatness. For many years Lawrence Brooks served as the chief judge of the Superior Court at Medford, watching the pageant of his country's politics flow by. He helped defend the victims of the famous "Red" raids of A. Mitchell Palmer after World War I and he has never been satisfied of the guilt of Sacco and Vanzetti. He quotes the remark Judge Thayer is said to have made to his golfing companions: "Did you see what I did to those Socialist bastards?" The evidence, Judge Brooks still feels, was far from convincing. He was the victim of a red-baiting campaign in the McCarthy days, but he doesn't mention this. Sue interjects to say: "He passed over a situation of devilish things." The Judge shrugs his shoulders and goes on to say he feels that since the First World War there has been a gradual downward trend in public morality.

The public, he believes, has become more and more tolerant of shady practices. His years on the bench have convinced him that juvenile delinquency is bred in homes, many of which are unfit in which to bring up children. He's not certain whether young people were morally better when he was growing up but sexual morality is much looser today. Whether that is good or bad is debatable.

"It never occurred to me when I was growing up," the Judge said, "that there was anything wrong with the world."

"I feel the world has grown worse since the end of the First World War," Sue says. "All of those young people taught to kill! I saw it."

What shocks her most is the race hatred in Boston and the fighting over the schools.

"It just makes me shudder," she says. "For over one hundred years we fought the battle. I am glad my father and mother are not alive to see Boston today."

At the root of it all, the Judge observes, is economics.

Sue recalls her father's dedication to the cause of the blacks.

"I think the reason that colored people are qualified as well as they are," she said, "is through the effort of the colored colleges. I think the result is showing now."

As for the future, the Judge says, he is a pessimist. He feels bad times lie ahead. He does not see how we can extricate ourselves from the environmental situation. We need all our resources and they are being consumed.

It is true that the world as a whole is better off than when he was a boy in the nineteenth century—just look at China, Russia and even India, but still he feels we are going to go down a long way before we go up again.

We would, he supposed, muddle through somehow but at the root of the problem is morality and economics. How are we going to prevent the wrong people—people like Nixon—from getting control? What makes me pessimistic, he says, is having to rely on the kind of people we do to guide us.

The Judge chuckles and the blue eyes in his weathered face sparkle.

"I don't worry myself about the theory that we aren't going to come out of all this. The ways of the Lord are devious and strange. Not that He is going to save us. I have no faith in those who say we are the chosen people. We have to find a way for ourselves or we are doomed."

Sue recalls a letter her mother wrote to a friend, a young man who'd lost his mother. She was ninety-two years old and in the letter she wrote: "There is a great mystery before me and a great hope."

The Judge expresses hope that the Republican Party, of which he is a faithful critic, "is not going to continue to be the party of the rich and stupid." As for the government and bureaucracy, like it or not, it is going to get bigger. He has little sympathy for conservative Republicans who think that we can return to McKinley. Ford, he thinks, is kidding himself if he really believes government can be cut back.

Eventually the country, he feels, will emerge from its difficulties. The law is changing noticeably and for the better. Education is changing for the better. In fifty years more or less things should be very different. He is certain the rich will not be as rich as now. Probably the inheritance laws will be revised and it will no longer be possible for men like Hunt and Getty to become billionaires and pass on such wealth to their descendants.

He did not think any other system of government was better than ours and of one thing was certain—young people today were far more mature than in his youth. Surely, there had been nothing like today's young people with their dedication to causes of justice and democracy when he was growing up.

The Judge talked a bit about his father who had been a Unitarian minister and who had wanted to enlist as a drummer boy in the Civil War. He even bought a drum and practiced drumming. But instead he followed in Thoreau's footsteps and walked down the Cape, even further than Thoreau, and got a job at Eastham as a schoolteacher. Finally, he left the ministry to devote his time to writing and speaking about the labor movement. Felix Frankfurter spoke at his funeral.

Yes, the Judge mused, we would get out of our difficulties. But it would take time and it would not be easy. The lack of public morality could not be brushed under the rug. When he thought of Saint-Gaudens' statue in the Boston Commons, dedicated to the black regiments that fought in the Civil War, and looked at what was going on among the Southies, this was the worst. To think that Boston, the City on the Hill, should come to that.

On a cool autumn day I stand before the Saint-Gaudens statue. Behind is the State House and its Golden Dome, the same whose stairs Hiram had climbed "to the cupelo" on a rainy November 19, 1817, one hundred and sixty years before me and looked out over Charleston, Castle Island, Dorchester Heights, the Glass House and the ship *Independence.* A banner: WE LOVE YOU RED SOX still waves rather forlornly. I walk over and inspect Saint-Gaudens' work. It is a bas-relief depicting Robert Gould Shaw, the commander of the black Fifty-fourth Massachusetts Volunteer infantry, formed in February, 1863, with his troops. The troops are mounted and someone has branded Shaw's horse with a heart in blue crayon. Each man's canteen bears a white star circled in blue and the saddle clothes are edged in blue. It is not a defacement, rather it is a homely touch applied by some street artist to relieve the heavy black of Saint-Gaudens' work. Beneath the statue three young people sit, two girls and a boy, workers from the State House or sightseers. They shift their places so that I can copy down the words engraved there: Death for Noble Deeds Makes Dying Sweet . . .

Now the circle is complete. I have retraced Hiram's footsteps and those of the family that emigrated westward. I have followed my own path from Minnesota out over the countryside which has been the domain of my reporting for the past quarter of a century.

What have I found? Not much of the physical world of Hiram and the first generation after the Revolution and only fragments of those middle years of pioneering that turned the continent to America's use. The houses and the mills vanish quickly in America. We have ravaged the land. I have found dark stains on the nation's fabric, pessimism and alienation, but I cannot entirely agree with a Russian friend of mine who knows the United States well. He feels the people are confused and the country is confused, that it has lost its way and that neither the nation or the people knows now what it wants. The United States, he says, has discovered that it is not as strong as it thought. When the Chinese told Kissinger that the United States was a wounded tiger they were right. It is still strong but it is a weakened tiger and he does not believe that we know how we will use our strength.

There is, I have found, confusion in the country, bitterness at lack of leadership, at the "lies", as Robert Bly has said, feeling that our heritage has been betrayed and I cannot argue that this is wrong. The heritage *has* been betrayed. High men *have* lied but that is only part of the coin. The farther I have traveled the more bright chips from the monuments of the past have turned up. No one can move through the granary states of mid-America and fail to be uplifted—certainly not one like myself, who began there. No one can talk to the possessors of the Minnesota spirit without catching its spark. I never expect to make peace with the new civilization of Pacifica, but I cannot ignore its sense of high adventure. Nor does New York resemble a dying city when I plunge into its depths and find men like Father Feeney bringing light to dark streets. The bloody heritage of the South now propounds an object lesson for the faint of heart and the feeble of purpose, black and white. If Birmingham can light a beacon there is hope enough for all. I come back to the City upon a Hill. It now broods in sullen hatred, but the example of Lawrence and Sue Brooks gives us an icon for our lives. "We shall overcome." We shall. In Boston. In all our Bostons.

I turn to a letter that came to me, postmarked Singapore, a few months ago, written by a young American who has read my book, *To Peking and Beyond*. He has lived in New England and California and often crossed the country by car. He went to Malaysia as a Peace Corps volunteer. He writes about his fellow Peace Corps members, not all young. One is seventy-one.

There is, he says, a quite unnoticed spirit in most of these people. This spirit is powerful.

"It was," he says, "forged in red blood in our long ago revolution when our forefathers aimed at the impossible by stating: All men are created Equal and have certain inalienable rights."

America, he believes, has always striven for high ideals while "an evil but definitely interesting self-made world tried to interfere."

"But despite greed, despite a strong sense of individualism," he writes. "America is rapidly moving towards a very exciting morning. The morning we all wake up equal and ourselves."

His friends, he says, are conservatives, radicals, midstreamers. They are environmentalists and entrepreneurs, socialists and capitalists.

"They are of every race," he writes, "they are all so different yet—all of us share something else which is quiet, unnoticed. It is what makes us Americans. We all believe, or at least a large percentage do, that we are created equal and can be free to be ourselves and although we might argue into the wee hours of the morning on some issue or other we respect each other and go to sleep not in hate but in friendship after argument.

"We are not defeated despite the government's now public attempt to subvert our spirit."

De Tocqueville said in 1835:

"Future events, whatever they may be, will not deprive the Americans of their climate or their inland seas, their great rivers or their exhuberant soil. Nor will bad laws, revolutions and anarchy be able to obliterate that love of prosperity and spirit of enterprise which seem to be the distinctive characteristic of their race or extinguish altogether the knowledge that guides them on their way."

I think I'll just let it stand at that. I cannot better catch the mood of our America as she steps forward into Century Three than in the words of these pages. De Tocqueville speaks for me. So do the young man in the Peace Corps, Lawrence and Sue Brooks, Mary Mebane and Cecil Roberts, Robert Bly and Muggsy Keeney, my old friends at North Side High, Father Feeney and Werner Thiers—all the people on these pages, Hiram and his generation. This is America. My America. I am an optimist and whatever they may say they are, too. So is America.

Index